W9-BRW-001

Advance Praise for *Your Anxious Child*

"In *Your Anxious Child*, Dacey and Fiore show parents and child care professionals how to recognize and alleviate the fears and anxieties that can inhibit social, emotional, and intellectual growth in children and teens. From monsters under the bed to bullies at the mall, social rejection to school phobia, separation anxiety to trips to the dentist—this practical, wise, and warm-hearted guide covers it all. With today's kids confronting an increasingly stressful world, *Your Anxious Child* is a book that every parent, teacher, and therapist needs to read and put into practice."

—**Alex J. Packer**, author, *Parenting One Day at a Time* and *How Rude! The Teenager's Guide to Good Manners, Proper Behavior, and Not Grossing People Out*; president, Freedom from Chemical Dependency Educational Services

"*Your Anxious Child* is a great place to begin for a parent (teacher, therapist, or pediatrician) who is seeking to understand and help a fearful child. The simple and straightforward style makes it easy to read and apply the complexity of thinking and the clinical and research experience underlying the ideas are very substantial. Learning to manage life's inevitable anxieties is one of the major tasks of childhood, and helping your child do this is one of the most satisfying aspects of parenthood. While psychotherapy and medication are available for severe situations, *Your Anxious Child* will help parents (and teachers) help children grow and develop in the vast majority of situations. I gladly recommend this delightful and persuasive book."

—**Timothy Dugan**, director of training in child and adolescent psychiatry, Cambridge City Hospital; psychiatry instructor, Harvard Medical School

"This book by experienced and distinguished therapists has well thought-out, tested strategies that not only reassure parents, but actually show them activities they can implement at home to help an anxious child."

—**Susan Shnidman**, psychotherapist and psychology instructor, Harvard Medical School

"*Your Anxious Child* is filled with hands-on advice and activities that can tell parents, teachers, therapists, and relatives specifically what to do to relieve phobias, separation and social fears, and general anxiety disorders. The ideas in this book have been researched extensively, so we can be sure they really work."
—**Neal Klein**, psychotherapist and associate professor, Lesley College

"Parents of anxious children and therapists who work with them and their families, as well as teachers and children, will benefit from this well researched, pragmatic program to treat those suffering from school, social, or generalized anxiety. The authors are authorities in the fields of developmental and educational psychology and well qualified in both research and clinical work. A clearly presented, easily accessible program."
—**Peggy E. Pressman**, clinical/educational psychologist in private practice

"Parents of anxious children will appreciate the emphasis that the authors of *Your Anxious Child* places on the parent-child relationship. Parents often feel helpless when it comes to helping their anxious children, but the activities in this book provide parents with tools that actually empower them. The authors' vignettes and quotes from parents who have used the COPE technique make this book enjoyable, and complement a most valuable resource."
—**Edwin Caine**, assistant clinical professor in child psychiatry, UCLA

"This holistic approach to anxiety is a practical, hands-on guide for professionals as well as parents. Who are these children? They sit in our classrooms every day manifesting their symptoms in a variety of ways that are sometimes unfathomable for the educator. Now, with the aid of *Your Anxious Child,* there are techniques and tools that can be implemented right away."
—**Korynne Taylor-Dunlop**, Curry College, M.Ed. program director and associate professor

Your
Anxious Child

John S. Dacey
Lisa B. Fiore

Your Anxious Child

How Parents and Teachers Can Relieve Anxiety in Children

with contributions by G. T. Ladd

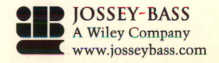
JOSSEY-BASS
A Wiley Company
www.josseybass.com

Published by

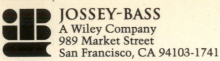

JOSSEY-BASS
A Wiley Company
989 Market Street
San Francisco, CA 94103-1741

www.josseybass.com

Copyright © 2000 by John Wiley & Sons, Inc.

FIRST PAPERBACK EDITION PUBLISHED IN 2002.

Jossey-Bass is a registered trademark of John Wiley & Sons, Inc.

"Typical Causes of Anxiety of Children at Several Age Levels" in Chapter One is reprinted from *Your Child's Emotional Health* by Philadelphia Child Guidance Center by permission of MacMillan.

No part of this publication may be reproduced, stored in a retrieval system, or transmitted in any form or by any means, electronic, mechanical, photocopying, recording, scanning, or otherwise, except as permitted under Sections 107 or 108 of the 1976 United States Copyright Act, without either the prior written permission of the Publisher or authorization through payment of the appropriate per-copy fee to the Copyright Clearance Center, 222 Rosewood Drive, Danvers, MA 01923, (978) 750-8400, fax (978) 750-4744. Requests to the Publisher for permission should be addressed to the Permissions Department, John Wiley & Sons, Inc., 605 Third Avenue, New York, NY 10158-0012, (212) 850-6011, fax (212) 850-6008, e-mail: permreq@wiley.com.

Jossey-Bass books and products are available through most bookstores. To contact Jossey-Bass directly, call (888) 378-2537, fax to (800) 605-2665, or visit our website at www.josseybass.com.

Substantial discounts on bulk quantities of Jossey-Bass books are available to corporations, professional associations, and other organizations. For details and discount information, contact the special sales department at Jossey-Bass.

We at Jossey-Bass strive to use the most environmentally sensitive paper stocks available to us. Our publications are printed on acid-free recycled stock whenever possible, and our paper always meets or exceeds minimum GPO and EPA requirements.

Library of Congress Cataloging-in-Publication Data
Dacey, John S.
   Your anxious child: how parents and teachers can relieve anxiety in children / John S. Dacey, Lisa B. Fiore. — 1st ed.
     p. cm.
     Includes bibliographical references and index.
     ISBN 0-7879-4997-3 (hard: alk. paper)
     ISBN 0-7879-6040-3 (paper)
     1. Anxiety in children. 2. Anxiety in adolescence. 3. Stress management in children. 4. Stress management in teenagers. 5. Parenting. I. Fiore, Lisa B., date. II. Title.
BF723.A5 D33 2000
649'.1—dc21
99–050517

HB Printing 10 9 8 7 6 5 4 3 2 1   FIRST EDITION
PB Printing 10 9 8 7 6 5

Contents

Acknowledgments   xi

1. What Anxiety Is and How It Can Be Alleviated   1

2. Eight Types of Anxiety Disorders in   25
   Children and Adolescents

3. COPE Step One: Calming the Nervous System   43

4. COPE Step Two: Originating an   85
   Imaginative Plan

5. COPE Step Three: Persisting in the   135
   Face of Obstacles and Failure

6. COPE Step Four: Evaluating and   165
   Adjusting the Plan

7. How Your Parenting Style Can Help   197
   Ease Your Child's Anxiety

Appendix A: Summary of Activities and   217
   Their Goals

Appendix B: Solutions to Activity Problems   225

Annotated Bibliography   227

About the Authors   233

Index   235

*This book is dedicated with deep affection
to some wonderful people:*

My sister, Margaret Lounsbery, a wise woman (JD).

*My forever teachers, Joan and Sanford Davidson,
Leonore Kelvin, who fed me apples, and Stephen Fiore,
who fills my heart (LF).*

Acknowledgments

The following people were kind enough to read all or parts of our manuscript and give us the benefit of their advice and editing: Jennifer Allen, Dr. Judith Arndell, Kristen Dacey, Linda Dacey, Mary Ellen Dacey, William Dacey, Terry DelPercio, Juliette Fay, Lisa Grandy, John Ladd, Stacey Phelan, Karen Philips, and Robin Tartaglia. We would also like to express our sincere gratitude to the parents in Natick, Massachusetts, Rancho Palos Verdes, California, and West Haven, Connecticut who participated in our most recent studies of the effectiveness of our methods.

We would also like to thank the folks at Jossey-Bass for all their hard work: Katie Crouch, Michele Jones, and Lasell Whipple. Most especially, we want to acknowledge that without the creativity, good writing sense, and friendly encouragement of our editor, Leslie Berriman, this book would have been much the poorer.

Your
Anxious Child

Chapter One

What Anxiety Is and How It Can Be Alleviated

Parents' Concerns

"My Katie is a little chatterbox, but when you ask her to perform, even for the family, she gets so nervous that she freezes up. I wish I could help her relax more."

"Almost since he was a baby, Jose has been a 'clinger.' He hated starting kindergarten, and even now in the third grade, he misses me and can't wait to get home. I can't travel anywhere without him. We thought up a plan to help him be less frightened, but it just didn't work out."

"Our Damian is terrified of animals. He hates to walk down the street by himself. He thinks a squirrel is going to jump out at him! We took him to a psychologist, who helped him think about his fears differently, and for while he was a lot better. Then a dog barked at him, and he just gave up."

"I wouldn't say Felicia is a frightened child. She does most of the things the other kids do—it's just that she worries about doing everything. She's very capable, but she's always afraid she's going to screw up. She works hard to get over her fears, and we tell her that she is doing better. She just can't see it, though. She just doesn't realize the improvements she's made."

These four parents' statements reflect the four central problems that all anxious children face:

1. They find it harder than other children to calm themselves when they are in a stressful situation.
2. Although many of them are above average in creativity, they seldom use this ability when making plans for coping with their anxiety.
3. Even when they do have a good plan, they tend to become discouraged with it after a while and often quit trying.
4. Even when they are making progress in reducing their anxious feelings, they fail to recognize their success.

It's hard to be the parent of an anxious child. Often you don't know what is causing her[1] anxiety, and sometimes you're not even aware that she is feeling frightened. Anxiety has been called the silent affliction, because most people are able to hide their upset from others. What can you as a parent do?

The good news is that studies have shown that about 90 percent of all anxious children can be greatly helped by learning coping skills. The goal of our book is straightforward: we want to empower you and your child with the coping skills that can help relieve her feelings of anxiety. In the chapters that follow, we will provide strategies and activities that you can use with your child to help her

---

[1] We have chosen to use the feminine pronoun *she* in the first chapter and will alternate it with *he* across the succeeding chapters.

understand and contend in new ways with being anxious. The strategies form the basis of our four-step COPE program, which has undergone fifteen years of successful field testing in schools and with individual children in various parts of the country. Each of the strategies that make up this program is accompanied by a set of activities. These activities will help you deal effectively with the four problems (listed earlier) that all anxious children face. COPE, which will be more fully described throughout this book, has been designed to ensure that all children are given opportunities to gain control over their anxiety problems, through the help of those who know and love them best: their parents.

Between 8 and 10 percent of American children and adolescents are seriously troubled by anxiety. Over three million children suffer from one (or more) of eight anxiety disorders; anxiety is currently the most prevalent psychiatric diagnosis in those sixteen and younger. Anxious children are two to four times more likely to develop depression, and as teenagers they are much more likely to become involved with substance abuse. Why? Are they victims of some trauma that has left them perpetually on guard? Were they just born that way? Are other factors involved?

As adults, most of us can look back on the worries of childhood and laugh at how insubstantial they appear. What once seemed like an iceberg now looks more like an ice cube. As grown-ups, we've all had life experiences that have given us the broader lens through which we can examine everyday worries and keep them in perspective. Unlike adults, children do not have those mental capabilities or that experience.

As parents, you are often faced with such questions from your child as "What if I'm not picked for the soccer team?" "What if I can't tie a square knot when it's my turn?" or "What if nobody gives me a valentine?" It is difficult to know whether your child's worries are a harmless case of the "what ifs" or whether she has a serious anxiety problem. For such a child, everyday tasks and events can become extremely challenging, with seemingly insurmountable obstacles. She simply can't imagine personal success when she first imagines failure or harm.

We're Never Going to Make It! (LF)[2]

It was a cold, sunny day as my father and I set out on our drive to the San Bernardino Mountains for my Indian Princesses retreat. This was a father-daughter group, similar to Cub Scouts or Girl Scouts, but based on Native American stories, crafts, and values. We were going camping with the other members of our group. We would be staying in real wood cabins, sleeping in cozy sleeping bags, and cooking food over a campfire. I had been looking forward to this trip for weeks, imagining ghost stories and marshmallows and looking up at a million stars in the night sky.

The drive was long, over two hours, and my father and I chatted about school, family, and life in general while we listened to the radio. Once we started the drive up the mountain, my attention was drawn away from conversation to the scenery outside my window. Sometimes the road curved sharply in hairpin turns, and I began to think that the two lanes seemed awfully narrow for two cars. On some stretches of roadway, there were only thin metal barriers on the edges of the cliffs, and on other parts of the road there were no barriers at all to prevent cars from falling thousands of feet to the ground below.

I began holding my breath when we drove around the sharp turns that were along the side of the cliffs, and felt great relief when we got back to the part of the road where my side was next to the mountain. Finally we turned off the main highway onto the local road that would take us to the campsite. There was no asphalt, only gravel, dirt, and

[2]When initials in parentheses appear after a story title, they indicate that the vignette was drawn from the life of one of the authors. All other vignettes are composites of stories of people who have been our clients or students.

ruts, which caused the car to bounce and bob as we drove slowly along, looking for the sign for our site.

"Do we have enough gas?" I asked my father. He assured me that we did, and kept driving. I tried to peek at the gas gauge to see where the needle was pointing, but I couldn't see it. I hoisted my seven-year-old body up higher, placing all of my weight on my wrists and elbows, and I could barely see the gauge. The needle didn't look right to me.

"Are you sure we've got enough gas?" I asked.

My father was beginning to get annoyed with me. "Yes, I said. We've got plenty of gas. Lisa, what are you doing? Sit down . . . and put your seat belt on," my father cautioned.

"It is on," I told him, and I continued to look at the gas gauge. I couldn't stop trying to see where the needle was, and I began holding my breath again. I imagined us being stuck in the middle of nowhere, and I would never see my mother or my brother again. We would die in the wilderness, and everyone would miss me.

"Finally," my father sighed. "Here we are!" We turned into the parking area of the campsite, and I recognized a few of my girlfriends from Indian Princesses. I felt the blood pumping through my heart as an enormous sense of relief flooded through me. "We made it!" I thought to myself. "Hooray!"

THE NATURE OF ANXIETY

Young Lisa certainly experienced some highly anxious moments on her trip with her father. From her father's view, she was never in any danger, but she imagined that she was. Do these feelings indicate that Lisa had a serious problem? Before we can try to answer this question, we need to further explain the nature of anxiety.

It is natural that children experience fear when they perceive a threat that may be real or imaginary. In fact, a moderate amount of fear can motivate them to learn new things. Whether the perceived threat takes the form of a dentist, a witch, or a snake, all children encounter stressful situations, and these circumstances change as the child matures into adolescence. For example, preschoolers may feel afraid of the dark, being alone, or monsters; older children may worry about rejection by peers or incompetence in school activities. Children and adolescents inevitably come to learn about potentially fearful, even dangerous, events. The ways they respond to anxiety depend on their individual personalities.

The terms *fear, worry,* and *anxiety* are often used interchangeably. In fact, there are subtle differences that are worth mentioning here. Psychologists use the word *fear* to describe frightened feelings toward a clear danger or threat. Fear is a reaction to an environmental threat that is focused on a specific object, individual, or circumstance. Worry is similar to fear, in that it refers to less intense reactions to specific dangers or foreboding about specific future events.

In contrast, anxiety is a general, frightened response to a source that is not readily identifiable. It could be the perception of a threat of what might have happened in the past or might happen in the future. An anxious child or adolescent may feel agitated and unsettled about some event over which she has no control. When a child is unable to think of a solution to the problem, feelings of helplessness often arise, resulting in a personal crisis. In summary, anxiety is a more generalized response to people or events that pose no immediate threat, although to the individual, they seem threatening.

WHEN ANXIETY BECOMES A PROBLEM

In the simplest sense, anxiety is the feeling that one's safety or well-being is threatened. Under some circumstances, a potential threat is readily resolved, such as the first time a child musters the courage to blow bubbles in the swimming pool. When she hears applause for joining the ranks of the "minnows," the threatened feeling is replaced by a feeling of success.

Some children, however, find it more difficult to experience success in everyday situations. They find themselves plagued by anxiety that is more pervasive than a simple fear. Most of the time, this feeling is the result of two types of mistaken thinking: (1) faulty perception of the facts and (2) misunderstanding of the meaning of the facts. (The child may experience one or both.) Let's look at some examples of mistaken thinking.

Fact: "My heart is beating faster than usual now."

Faulty perception of the fact: "My heart is racing; it feels like it may burst!"

Misunderstanding of the meaning of the fact: "If my heart rate doesn't slow down soon, I will surely have a heart attack and die!"

Other typical faulty perceptions of facts: "This distressing situation is really always going to be this way." "No one understands me." "I am a totally weak person."

Other typical misunderstandings of the meaning of facts: "Because I am having tense and fearful feelings, I am unlucky. Maybe I deserve this stress. Others don't have it. I must be getting punished for something I've done." "I'm so often scared, there must be something wrong with me. I have some sickness [devil, syndrome, demon, mental illness] in me that won't let me rest." "I can see no real danger, but still I feel fearful; obviously I am missing some threat to my safety."

For your child's anxiety to be reduced or eliminated, these errors in thinking must be rectified. The goal of all the strategies and activities in this book is to help your child achieve this end. However, this book should not replace psychotherapy and medical treatment for the more serious cases. The only safe way you can determine the seriousness of your child's problem is through the professional methods used by qualified therapists and psychiatrists. Nevertheless, it is our contention that you, the parent, are most often in the best position to help, especially when you are armed with the knowledge available in this book.

MAJOR CAUSES OF ANXIETY

Social scientists used to try to explain human traits, including anxiety, from the standpoint of two causes: nature and nurture—that is, genes and environment. In recent years, social scientists have carried out numerous studies of the causes of anxiety. They have made much headway. Perhaps the most important conclusion they have reached is that anxiety always results from a combination of three factors: biological, psychological, and social. These researchers use what is referred to as the *biopsychosocial model* to explain the influence and interrelationships of the three factors. Understanding this model will help you take a more comprehensive approach to coping with your child's problems. Let's look at each of these factors more closely. Although we describe them separately, please remember that in reality they are always interacting and affecting each other.

Biological Factors

From the moment your child was conceived, she was subject to biological influences that affected her level of anxiety. Some of the indicators of a genetic tendency toward anxiety are obvious, such as a tense, irritable temperament or erratic sleep patterns. Other biological factors are less obvious but are equally influential, such as hormonal imbalances and abnormal brain activity. Whenever these biological abnormalities are present, they increase adrenaline in the bloodstream. As a result, a child will likely exhibit some physiological symptoms: shallow breathing, increased heart rate, sweaty palms, and tense muscles, for example. These symptoms are also typical when a child or adolescent is under stress and experiences the *alarm reaction*. The alarm reaction involves twenty-two physiological responses that usually result from heightened adrenaline levels (see the list that follows). Not all of these responses need to occur simultaneously for the alarm reaction to be present. Ironically, many people come to fear the uncomfortable and disabling symptoms of the alarm reaction more than the cause of the anxiety itself.

Physiological Responses of the Alarm Reaction

1. Increased heart rate
2. Sweating
3. Hyperventilation (faster, shallower breathing)
4. Constriction of some blood vessels, dilation of others
5. Feeling faint, dizzy (as blood moves away from extremities, especially the head, to the center of the body)
6. Dry mouth from decreased salivation
7. Higher "squeaky" voice from tightness in throat
8. Sharper eyesight from dilated pupils
9. Queasy feeling resulting from inflamed intestinal lining
10. Decreased digestive ability
11. Decreased interest in food
12. Decreased verbal ability, sometimes including stuttering and stammering
13. Increased blood-clotting ability
14. Onset of the "fight-or-flight" mechanism in the subcortex of the brain
15. Increased motor ability
16. Decreased mental ability, sometimes including indecision
17. Raising of hair on the back of the neck (makes animals with fur look bigger)
18. Excitation of muscle fibers, sometimes to the point of trembling (for example, knees)
19. Increased pallor of skin, especially of the face
20. Decreased interest in sex
21. Hypervigilance
22. An overall feeling of tension

Physiological factors such as sleep, stimulation, and food affect the anxiety response to a degree and on an individual basis. For example, your child may be getting too much stimulation from her environment or not enough. Any child will be more easily agitated if she has not had enough sleep or has ingested too many candy bars or sugary, caffeinated soft drinks. Exercising judgment and control over a child's sleeping and eating habits is easier with young children than with adolescents, who make more decisions on their own. Nevertheless, by modeling desired eating habits and sleeping routines in the home, you can beneficially influence your child both directly and indirectly.

Psychological Factors

Psychological causes of anxiety result from an interaction between biological forces and disturbing experiences. An example would be what happens when a child takes a tumble off a tricycle. For most children it is upsetting, but they soon forget it. For a child who has a "high-wired" nervous system, however, such an accident can cause tricycles to become feared objects. Psychological factors affect the way your child perceives and thinks about the world.

Children who are anxious also become hypervigilant, which is a heightened state of sensitivity to the *possibility* of danger or threat. If your child's mind is in a constant state of alert, you may have discovered that she finds it difficult to relax. If your child views the world hypervigilantly, she is likely to spend most of her time in a state of discomfort, which in turn distorts her view of reality.

Social Factors

Social factors typically involve your child's interactions with her family and friends and others in her life. These people may contribute to her anxiety in various ways, and their influences change as she matures. Parents, siblings, and other playmates can be constant sources of anxiety if she perceives them as a threat. For example, her big brother may be only kidding, but your child may think he is really going to hurt her. The intentions of these persons may be good, but if your child is predisposed toward feelings of anxiety, then everyday conflicts may seem especially threatening to her.

The patterns of behavior that parents use in raising their children are referred to as *parenting style*. Several such styles have been identified, and each contributes, positively or negatively, to children's development. Some parents, for example, demand perfection from their children. Such children may come to believe that their efforts can never be good enough. These circumstances can foster serious problems, such as eating disorders. Having an anxious parent or sibling often contributes to a child's level of anxiety, particularly if the parent or sibling shares his own anxieties with the child. When the child sees her role model in a state of anxiety, she may come to internalize these feelings herself.

We do not wish to convey the idea that if a child is anxious, it is the parents' fault. Parents can, of course, contribute to the problem, but many studies show that children are influenced by many aspects of their environment, and parents are only one of them. We will explore the ways that parenting style can encourage freedom from anxiety in Chapter Seven.

As you will see in the section that follows, different cultures can also produce a myriad of unique influences. A good example of the importance of social context may be seen in the children of the Caribbean islands. Consider the views of two therapists who practice on one of these islands, St. Maarten, which is about one hundred miles east of Puerto Rico. Dr. Karen Philips was born in Holland and has worked on St. Maarten as a clinical psychologist for the last sixteen years. Dr. Judith Arndell was born on St. Maarten and has spent most of her life there.

Anxiety Among Caribbean Children

Dr. Philips observes that after hurricane Luis, which brought about major destruction on St. Maarten in September 1995, the number of posttraumatic stress cases increased. She sees the source of her clients' anxiety as their anticipation of their surroundings, as well as the way they talk silently to themselves about their perceptions. Focusing on changing this "inner talk" toward more positive statements and anticipations is the core of her plan for treating these anxieties. If clients realize they can actively change their own perceptions and thoughts, then a sense of control develops that can result in reducing anxiety. The choice is whether to concentrate on and emphasize what could go wrong or what could go right. Dr. Philips finds that if her clients can focus more positively and constructively on developing healthier inner talk instead of fighting anxiety, they can make good progress.

Dr. Arndell states that more than half of her clients suffer from anxiety problems. She finds that in Caribbean children and teens, stormy weather is certainly a problem. However, she believes their primary problem is the insecurity caused by their parents telling them they will be punished by spiritual beings (bogeymen, devils, their dead relatives) for their bad behavior. The youngsters come to believe that these hobgoblins hide in various places, waiting to punish them.

"As a result," Dr. Arndell says, "the children frequently develop fears of going into certain rooms, especially bathrooms and bedrooms. Many of them become obsessed with these concerns. Such obsessions often lead to separation anxiety, performance anxiety, and a variety of social phobias. They can be quite difficult to overcome. In fact, comparing my ten years' experience in the United States and the rest of my career here, I would say that although the causes of the problems of Caribbean children and American children are often different, the ways they manifest their anxiety are really quite similar.

"I see my job as helping kids to stop thinking about all those negative things in their lives, whether real or imaginary. I teach them not to entertain those thoughts. I show them how to substitute more wholesome ideas. Most of my younger clients need to practice having thoughts about safety and security. That's what I tell their parents, too: 'If you can make them feel that their home is secure, that's the most important contribution you can make to relieving their anxiety.'

"The other thing I emphasize is living in the present. Most of these kids have their minds fixed firmly on what is going to happen. I try to help them quiet their fears about what the future will bring and instead to concentrate on the present moment. When I can get them to do that, they're on their way to getting better."

In the Caribbean, virtually all children have experienced hurricanes and have been threatened by the idea of bogeymen. Most do not suffer from anxiety problems, however. Those who do usually are also afflicted with highly sensitive temperaments, have experienced early psychological distress, and lack effective social supports such as belonging to a close circle of friends. No matter what the behavior, it is always the result of the complex interaction of these three factors. This combination of biological, psychological, and social elements is a good example of what we mean by the biopsychosocial model.

ANXIETY AT DIFFERENT AGES AND STAGES

As you may well have noticed, age affects your child's anxiety patterns. For example, infants' fears revolve around sensory experiences, such as loud noises, falls, and their parents' absence. Toddlers will likely experience fear of strangers or distress upon their caregivers' departure (known as separation anxiety). Childhood brings with it fears of animals, the dark, and imaginary beasts and creatures. As children's circles of exploration and experience widen, the likelihood of exposure to anxiety-provoking stress increases. Children in middle childhood are often concerned with performance, and adolescents are more concerned with social and interpersonal anxieties as they begin to form intimate relationships. The list that follows shows the typical fears that child experts find at several age levels.

Typical Causes of Anxiety of Children at Several Age Levels

Ages	Causes of Anxiety
6 to 7	Strange, loud, or abrupt noises (for example, animal noises, telephone and alarm ringing, wind and thunder sounds)
	Ghosts, witches, and other "supernatural" beings
	Separation from parents and being lost
	Being alone at night (and having nightmares or visitations from "evil" creatures)
	Going to school (so-called school phobia)
	Physical harm from, or rejection by, specific individuals at school
7 to 8	The dark and dark places (such as closets, attics, and basements)
	Real-life catastrophes suggested by television, the movies, and books (for example, kidnaping, floods, fires, nuclear attack)
	Not being liked
	Being late for school or left out of school or family events
	Physical harm from or rejection by specific individuals at school
8 to 9	Personal humiliation
	Failure in school or play
	Being caught in a lie or misdeed
	Being the victim of physical violence (either from known people or from strangers; either deliberately or randomly motivated)
	Parents fighting, separating, or being hurt
9 to 11	Failure in school or sports
	Becoming sick
	Specific animals (especially animals larger than humans or those known to attack humans)

                Heights and sensation of "vertigo" (for example, dizziness)

                Sinister people (for examples, killers and molesters)

11 to 13   Failure in school, sports, or social popularity

                Looking and acting "strange"

                Death or life-threatening illness or disease

                Sex (attracting others, repelling others, being attacked)

                Being fooled or "brainwashed"

                Losing possessions, being robbed

The famed child expert Jean Piaget proposed that children's thinking proceeds from vague to specific awareness of their surroundings. Then, in early adolescence, the child's thinking progresses from concrete to abstract ideas. As a child's mental abilities evolve, her capacity for anticipating the future improves. This enables her to meet the increasingly complex demands of the tasks she encounters. Unfortunately, a downside to this growth is the improved ability to clearly visualize the possibility of unpleasant events. Normal fears become associated with exaggerated expectations. Thus some youngsters become progressively more anxious as they move toward adolescence.

CURRENT THERAPEUTIC PERSPECTIVES ON ANXIETY

The science of psychology has taught us a great deal about the nature of anxiety. Unfortunately, but not surprisingly, there is still some disagreement about the best way to reduce it. There are several schools of thought that influence diagnosis and treatment of anxiety in children and adolescents: psychoanalytic, behaviorist, family systems, and cognitive. We think it is important to briefly describe these current psychotherapeutic viewpoints so that you can clearly see the orientation of this book. Many of the activities you

will do later in the book are built on these perspectives, especially
the behaviorist, family systems, and cognitive viewpoints. Also,
knowing this information is helpful when you are choosing a therapist, should that be necessary.

The Psychoanalytic Perspective

Although Sigmund Freud was the father of psychoanalysis, his
work has been largely superseded by the theory of Erik Erikson,
another famous psychoanalyst. In his much-discussed book *Childhood and Society*, Erikson outlined eight universal stages of development. He stated that progressing from one stage to the next
depends on the child's resolving the conflict present in each stage.
At each stage, two personality traits conflict with each other. For
example, at stage two the conflict is between whether the child
develops a sense of autonomy or becomes filled with a sense of
shame. For healthy development, the child needs to resolve the
crisis in favor of the first trait in each pair. From the standpoint of
the anxious child, the most relevant stage is stage four: industry
versus inferiority. During this stage, which occurs at approximately
five to eleven years of age, children are concerned with performance in school and at home. The anxious child may be overly
concerned with "making the grade" both academically and socially.
"Will I pass the test?" "Will I make new friends?" "Are people making fun of me behind my back?"

For these children, anxiety exceeds the routine self-doubts that
others experience. An anxious child is often hindered because her
anxiety is so great that she has difficulty functioning with her peers.
When this happens, she experiences a sense of inferiority, and her
ability to achieve success declines.

Psychoanalysis tries to help children primarily through encouraging them to express their anxious feelings and then analyzing the
origins of these feelings. A major emphasis of this perspective is the
relationship between the parents and the child. Through a process

called transference, a therapist attempts to act as a surrogate parent and to help the child restructure her feelings about herself by being a kind and understanding parent-substitute.

The Behaviorist Perspective

Anxious children naturally wish to avoid situations that scare them, even more than other children do. When your child avoids such situations, her behavior is reinforced because her frightened feelings are temporarily reduced. This only perpetuates the anxiety, according to behaviorist theorists, such as B. F. Skinner. Some parents feel that giving in to the child's reluctance is appropriate and caring, but doing so enables the child to avoid fearful situations, and she thus fails to deal with the problem.

Another aspect of the behaviorist approach is seen in the work of Albert Bandura, who has done considerable research on the concept of modeling. Stating that children learn primarily through imitation and modeling, Bandura espouses the use of these processes to promote confident behaviors in children. In modeling situations, parents or other influential individuals behave calmly and competently in real or make-believe scary scenarios, which shows the child alternative reactions to anxious situations. According to this perspective, you instruct your child to imitate what you do, then give her positive feedback as she succeeds in doing so. Over time, she learns to adopt these modeled behaviors as her own and gradually becomes less anxious.

The Family Systems Perspective

Family systems therapists, such as Virginia Satir, regard the anxiety symptoms of an individual as a family problem, and thus they find it necessary to treat the whole family rather than just the child or adolescent. There are many varieties of family treatments, which may be combined in different ways and with other types of therapy.

Perhaps the most important feature of this perspective is the idea of bringing the whole family together for therapeutic sessions, as families are seen as self-sustaining systems that influence each member in a myriad of ways. The child is the "identified patient" whose symptoms bring the family to therapy. Once the family's rituals, rules, and routines have been determined, the therapist attempts to alter the patterns that affect the child. These changes then reverberate throughout the family system. For example, a family therapist will try to influence the interactions between a husband and wife in order to help the child. The personal story that follows illustrates how a mother's anxieties about separation from her husband can affect her children.

The Attack of the River Rats (JD)

Our house had a small front yard, surrounded by a low hedge. On the side of the hedge facing away from our house was a huge open field sloping down to the railroad tracks and the bank of the Delaware River. There was a narrow break in the hedge that opened onto a path, and that path led across the field to a train station about a quarter-mile away. It was exactly the kind of place that kids would want to explore and that any parent would declare off-limits.

My mother could not help worrying about it all the time; she was a "worry wart." Her training as a nurse contributed to this trait, I think. She was perpetually concerned that the colds my brothers and I were always catching would turn into pneumonia and that our bumps on the head had caused concussions. She felt sure that one day one of us would wander through the hedge, cross the field, and get hit by a train. To prevent this, she told us a vivid story about the "river rats":

"You kids must never go through that hedge unless Daddy or I am with you. A family of river rats lives down by the river, and there are always a few of them hiding near the opening of the hedge. They have a cave in the riverbank, and they might take you there. If you become their pet, they won't let you come home again. So if you know what's good for you, you'd better stay away from that hedge!"

Her story was effective, particularly because there really were immense rats in that area. I still have a most graphic memory of the few that occasionally made their way into our house. And so we children were duly terrified by the thought of crossing through that hedge. But I don't recall my siblings becoming hypervigilant as I did—on the lookout for danger everywhere. Therefore, my mother didn't *cause* me to be a highly anxious child. I believe I had inherited an inclination toward an anxious personality. Early experiences, such as this rat situation, interacted with my genetic proclivity to produce a "nervous" child—me.

One morning when I came downstairs for breakfast, I found my mother entering the front door, wearing her light coat and a hat with one of those veils made so popular during the war years by Ingrid Bergman and the other mysterious Hollywood femmes fatales. I couldn't see her face, so at first I didn't realize that she was sobbing. When I did, I asked her what was wrong.

"Oh, nothing. I just walked Daddy to catch a train, and I'm just very sad that he's gone." I later learned that she hated it when my father traveled.

It was unusual that my father should take a train trip, but he had done so before. Nevertheless, she had said the word *gone,* and the first thought that occurred to my four-year-old mind was that the rats had gotten him. I pictured hundreds of rats jumping on my father from their hiding places in the hedge. They knocked him to the ground and, with pieces of his clothing clenched in their teeth, dragged him back to their disgusting cave. I started crying too, and it took her a while to discover my fear. Eventually, she helped me calm down, but this was one more reinforcement for me that life is a very dangerous undertaking. It was years before I began to question that attitude.

The Cognitive Perspective

The cognitive perspective on anxiety focuses on the *thoughts* of the child. This view is the opposite of the psychoanalytic approach, which identifies repressed feelings as the culprits. Cognitivists, such as Aaron Beck, believe it is distorted thinking that causes disruptive feelings rather than the other way around. In the cognitive view, feelings are analogous to the level of the mercury in the thermometer when you have a fever. The heightened mercury in the thermometer is not itself important. It simply indicates that the body's internal temperature is above average, which is a sign of an invasion of germs. So it is with anxious feelings: they usually reflect thought patterns that have gone awry. Fix the thoughts, and the anxious feelings will subside.

Your child plays an active part in controlling her life through the way she thinks about things. For example, confronting unfamiliar situations is probably quite anxiety provoking for her. For some children, novel situations are not bothersome, but for anxious children, novelty can fuel an already anxious temperament. For them, if it's new, it's dangerous.

One way to make your child less likely to perceive situations as threatening is through "cognitive restructuring." This treatment involves working with her to

- Remove or reduce misinterpretations of reality

- Challenge faulty logic or irrational self-statements

- Construct a way of looking at the world that includes adaptive coping strategies (much more on this in Chapter Four)

The Perspective We Espouse

In our work with children and adolescents, we have employed each of these four perspectives. Although there are cases that respond well to the psychoanalytic, behaviorist, and family systems perspectives, in our experience most anxiety problems can best be helped by the cognitive orientation. Anxious children tend to be brighter than average and therefore are more likely to understand the mental skills the cognitive approach is trying to foster. In addition, as we argued earlier in this chapter, anxiety itself is most often a result of faulty perceptions and, even more important, faulty interpretations of the facts. Cognitive therapy is specifically designed to discover and correct mental misapprehensions. Therefore, the COPE program consists mainly of activities that were inspired by this orientation.

THE COPE METHOD

For the past fifteen years, John Dacey has been experimenting with techniques for helping children and adolescents increase their self-control over their study habits and their ability to avoid using drugs. In recent years he has adapted this method specifically to help children with anxiety problems. The method that has resulted from all this research is called *COPE*. The letters in this acronym stand for the four steps that make up the method:

1. C = Calming the nervous system
2. O = Originating an imaginative plan
3. P = Persisting in the face of obstacles and failure
4. E = Evaluating and adjusting the plan

What we have discovered through our teaching and our therapeutic and research studies is that most people, children and adults, have similar problems when they deal with situations that are anxiety provoking. These four problems (the same ones that are reflected in the four quotations with which we opened this chapter) fall into categories that are the focus of the four steps of COPE.

Calming the Nervous System

The first problem most of us confront when we enter a stressful situation is the stimulation of the fight-or-flight response, a physiological reaction to assault that is "hard-wired" into the human body.
In prehistoric times this response, which prepares the body either
to attack the antagonist or to run away, was most functional; life-
or-death situations demanded immediate, unthinking action. In
those days, if you were out hunting alone and saw an enemy tribe
running toward you, pausing to consider your alternatives could
mean disaster. Today, however, children in most scary situations
cannot resolve their problems by simply attacking or running away.
For example, as your child walks into a room full of children at a
birthday party, she may feel angry with the people staring at her, or
she may want to run and hide. However, what she needs to do is
quell this neurological response to stress so that she can think
clearly about what she wants to say and how she wants to say it. A
calm nervous system, then, not a highly aroused one, is what she
needs when dealing with most modern stressors.

In this book we will cover different strategies for calming the
nervous system. Some of them are physical, some mental, some a
combination of the two, and some involve spiritual approaches. We
will provide numerous activities that your child may use to achieve
tranquility.

Originating an Imaginative Plan

The second problem that anxious people often face is that, even
when calm, they often have faulty understandings of their feelings
and why they have them. Further, because they are under such pressure, they may be unable to think of really imaginative plans for
dealing with their quandaries. Anxious children are less likely than
others to have imaginative ideas about the best way to problem-
solve, even though, with their vibrant imaginations, they often have

greater creative potential. However, if they have calmed down their nervous systems, they can use the techniques that we teach to originate better insights about themselves and design an imaginative plan for dealing with their problem.

In recent years, research has identified a number of thinking strategies and styles that are much more likely to produce creative problem solving. We will offer numerous activities that are aimed at helping you and your child become better problem solvers. As you and she learn these techniques, you both will improve your ability to design a plan that will really combat her anxiety.

Persisting in the Face of Obstacles and Failure

We have found that many plans for dealing with anxiety start out well, but then the child loses faith. The temptation to quit blossoms, and soon the child gives up on her plan. A number of scholars have shown that those people who believe in God or some other higher power or supernatural force such as the Great Spirit are more likely to persevere when the going gets tough. Anxious children are especially prone to the problem of "throwing in the towel." We will offer a variety of paths your child can take to help her have faith in herself, her plan, and her "higher power." Among these paths is a new one about which we are very excited: techniques for designing your own family rituals, which, when faithfully attended to, are proving to be powerful anxiety fighters.

Evaluating and Adjusting the Plan

Having faith in her plan is important, but what is critical to your child's success is making sure the plan really works. We recommend evaluation techniques to use both while the plan is in operation and after the plan has been carried out, so that you and your child can construct improvements. We suggest a number of ways your child can get objective feedback on the efficacy of her plan.

We have devoted a chapter to each of these four strategies. In these chapters, we offer activities that will help you and your child practice the strategy and see precisely how to carry it out. Some of these activities are for five- to ten-year-olds, some are for ten- to seventeen-year-olds, and some are useful for this whole age range. Why have we chosen these ages? We start with five-year-olds because we believe that our cognitive approach is too difficult for children younger than that. Many of our activities would be helpful for persons older than seventeen, but we assume that most of them will no longer be under parental guidance in their efforts to quell their anxiety problems.

Chapter Two

Eight Types of Anxiety Disorders in Children and Adolescents

Just a Case of Stage Fright? (JD)

When I was twelve, I was an altar boy at the Catholic church in my neighborhood. In March, I had been told that I had been selected to be one of the altar boys for the High Mass on Easter morning—a great honor. I was excited but also very nervous, for I knew that most of my friends would see me up there. As the day drew near, I became filled with a sense of dread, fearing that I would surely make some terribly embarrassing mistake and that all my friends would laugh at me. On the morning of Easter Sunday, I awoke very early and, overwhelmed with anxiety, went to the bathroom and vomited. With no breakfast I left the house and slowly walked to Saint Thomas's Church.

I was sure that prisoners trudging along death row to their executions felt no worse than I did. I stood in front of a sink in the altar boys' room, splashing water on my face, hoping for a last-minute reprieve—maybe the mass would be canceled, maybe there'd be a fire alarm, maybe, just maybe the fear would go away. It didn't. Finally it was eleven o'clock, and the time for a miracle had passed. With the other altar boys, I followed the three priests who were celebrating the mass out to the sacristy of the church.

I stole a glance at the congregation and saw several of my friends in the tightly packed crowd. The church felt very warm, and the stiff collar I was wearing was becoming tighter by the minute. Then it happened. The bright lights began to fade, the altar seemed to move upward, and I fainted.

I took some ribbing about the incident from my male friends, but nothing that justified the severe sense of mortification I felt. It was so strong that for several years I could hardly bear to speak in class, and whenever I was supposed to make a presentation, I would feign illness. I grew disgusted with myself, hating my unmanly lack of confidence. Finally, in the ninth grade, I was nominated for class president, and, determined to overcome my trepidation, I ran for and won the election.

Being president also meant being the MC of the school assemblies. The first time I had to do it was awful, but somehow I made it through. The next several assemblies were better. To my amazement, I actually began to enjoy the role. After all my terrors, this was a welcome change.

In the last assembly of the school year, the glee club was to sing a variety of inspiring songs. I had begun to feel so confident that I memorized the selections I was to announce, so that I would not have to read them from a card. I knew it was showing off, but it was such an exhilarating feeling, especially compared to my Easter Sunday experience. I did place a card with the selections printed on it under my chair, just in case. All went well until the fifth song. I stood before the microphone to announce it and realized I could not remember its name or its composer.

The usual buzz of whispers and giggles quickly came to a halt, as though the volume control on a radio was being turned down. I'm sure no more than thirty seconds went by, but the expectant silence seemed to last for an hour. Mercifully, the title of the selection came to me, and in a shaky voice I announced it, making no mention of the forgotten composer's name. Before the last two selections, I surreptitiously retrieved the card from under my seat and glanced at the information so that this debacle would not happen again.

After the assembly, five teachers came up to me. "Boy, I'm in for it now," I thought, but they proceeded to pat me on the back and congratulate me. "Thank you very much," I said, beaming, pretending I knew what it was all about. "We're so proud of you," one of them told me enthusiastically. "Why, you're the first president we can remember who's had the courage to wait until the students were quiet before he would announce the next selection!"

At last, I thought, this phobia is beaten. It wasn't. In the years to come, I was an anxious speaker on numerous occasions. But this early victory was evidence that improvement is possible if you are willing to stick your neck out.

This personal vignette describes one of the more common anxiety disorders: social phobia. *Disorder* may sound like a harsh word, even implying mental disturbance. To psychologists, however, it simply refers to conditions that seriously interfere with ordinary behavior and that continue for more than a short time. John, for example, didn't just have stage fright—he was incapable of public speaking for several years.

We believe it is important for you to know about the eight different types of anxiety disorders that can occur in children and adolescents. We think that if you are able to differentiate between these different types, you will have several important advantages as you try to help your child:

- Your thinking about your child's problem will be sharpened by the descriptions of the eight anxiety disorders.

- You will be better able to discuss your child's condition with professionals and other parents. In the field of psychology, there are many misunderstood terms. (For example, many people use the term *paranoid*, which is a serious schizophrenia, when they merely mean *suspicious.*) In many ways, it will pay to know and use these terms accurately.

- It may relieve some of your own anxiety to know more specifically whether your child has one of these disorders (although only a professional can tell you for certain).

- Because you will have a clearer definition of your child's problem, you may be better able to help your child with each of the steps of the COPE program. For example, suppose your child has separation anxiety; that is, he hates to be away from his family, so he often refuses to go to school. Knowing something about this syndrome could help you apply each of the COPE steps better:

  Calm the nervous system—you might design a visualization system (see Chapter Three).

  Originate an imaginative plan—you could instruct your child in writing down his feelings about how each hour of his day is going (see Chapter Four).

  Persist in the face of obstacles and failure—you could strengthen the reward structure by including more "private time" with Mom (see Chapter Five).

  Evaluate and adjust the plan—you might help your child record his "resistance to leaving home" ratings; the less resistance, the less separation anxiety (see Chapter Six).

In this chapter we will describe the eight major categories of anxiety disorder:

1. Specific (simple) phobia
2. Social phobia
3. Agoraphobia

4. Panic disorder
5. Generalized anxiety disorder (GAD)
6. Separation anxiety
7. Posttraumatic stress disorder (PTSD)
8. Obsessive-compulsive disorder (OCD)

All eight of these anxiety disorders can be found among children and adolescents. It is important to remember, however, that sometimes more than one of these disorders may occur at the same time, making it difficult to identify a single disorder.

SPECIFIC (SIMPLE) PHOBIA

A specific phobia is an intense anxiety in the face of a circumstance or object that in reality poses no danger. Specific phobias can be divided into several broad types, including animal type (animals or insects), natural environment type (thunder, wind, heights, and so on), blood-injection-injury type (seeing blood, getting a shot, and so on), situational type (flying, tunnels, bridges, and so on), and others. Table 2.1 lists the names of representative specific phobias.

Common among young children, these phobias generally are not debilitating and tend to disappear as the child gets older. However, for some children and adolescents, specific phobias that are not adjusted can be debilitating and can limit normal functioning. Specific phobias may become a central part of a child's daily life if he feels that he has to avoid those things that make him anxious. This behavior can be a source of tremendous frustration and discomfort for the child and his family.

Another important consideration when investigating whether a child struggles with a phobia is whether or not a specific phobia has developed as a secondary problem following a trauma. For example, a child who sustained a serious injury as a result of a car accident might become afraid of riding in a car; a child who was injured

Table 2.1. Types of Specific Phobias.

Animal	Natural	Blood-Injection-Injury	Situational	Other
Gataphobia (fear of cats)	Hylophobia (fear of forests)	Hypochondria (fear of getting sick)	Harpaxophobia (fear of robbers)	Chronophobia (fear of clocks)
Zoophobia (fear of animals)	Chionophobia (fear of snow)	Necrophobia (fear of death)	Erythrophobia (fear of blushing)	Triakaidekaphobia (fear of the number thirteen)
	Astraphobia (fear of thunderstorms)		Acrophobia (fear of high places)	Pantrophobia (fear of almost everything)
	Amapthophobia (fear of dust)			

by a dog might become anxious around animals. It is important to differentiate between these kinds of reactions, which may be part of posttraumatic stress disorder (discussed later), and specific phobias without a history of trauma. This distinction is important: specific phobias can usually be treated by such strategies as those in this book; PTSD always requires treatment by a professional.

SOCIAL PHOBIA

A child or adolescent with a social phobia experiences persistent anxiety in social situations. Because he believes that he will perform badly, he consistently focuses on the threat of embarrassment. Certain social situations may cause more anxiety than others. For example, he may have no problem asking for directions from a teacher, yet he may be terrified to speak in his classroom.

Although social phobias tend to emerge during adolescent years, they can also be found in children who are excessively shy. Certainly shyness is a normal part of any child's or adolescent's life, as are feelings of uneasiness around strangers. However, this otherwise normal behavior can cause problems when the child's desire to avoid strangers, including people his own age, becomes so extreme that it interferes with the child's school performance and social life.

Children with social anxiety often realize that their fear is exaggerated, but they still cannot control it. This can be very frustrating and scary, because this lack of control over their own emotions may make them even more anxious. In order to regulate themselves emotionally, social phobics will tend to avoid many social situations. If left unresolved, social phobia and the anxiety it gives rise to may lead to a sense of frustrating isolation and depression.

Sadly, some younger children avoid the social world by shutting themselves out verbally. This is a symptom of social phobia called selective mutism. The child is unable to speak in some social situations but speaks well enough in other situations. Selective mutism usually begins when children are very young and may extend into adolescence if untreated.

AGORAPHOBIA

A child will be diagnosed with agoraphobia rather than social phobia when his anxiety is so severe that he is unable to participate in most social situations. Nearly twenty-five hundred years ago, the Greek physician Hippocrates noticed that some people became very nervous in the marketplace (*agora* in Greek), and he named the condition *agoraphobia*. Actually, the phobia has more to do with an excessive worry about losing control of one's self in one's surroundings. Thus, in extreme cases, agoraphobics become housebound because home is the only place they can feel safely in control of themselves.

Sometimes simple phobias can mask agoraphobia. For example, a twelve-year-old boy may have a fear of germs, so he avoids school buses, parks, and any other public settings where he thinks it is possible that he might come in contact with germs. This boy may be an agoraphobic who focuses his anxiety on germs in order to avoid what he really is afraid of: losing control in public places.

Agoraphobia is not common among young children and typically begins to establish itself among adolescents or young adults. However, therapists have found that the symptoms of agoraphobia can begin to show themselves even among young children. Agoraphobic children and adolescents experience strong anxiety when they find themselves in circumstances in which they feel vulnerable. They tend to believe that it will be difficult to depart an uncomfortable situation or that they will be criticized for leaving, so they begin to dwell on feelings of being trapped or exposed. Therapists often summarize the complicated feelings agoraphobics experience as "fear of fear."

As a consequence of their avoidance of frightened feelings, agoraphobics may withdraw to settings in which they feel safe: their home, a specific route to school, or certain homes of friends or relatives, for example. They avoid places that to others may seem safe and comfortable, such as school, crowded places, classrooms without windows, the backseat of a car, tunnels, and limited-access roads. For most agoraphobic children and adolescents, home is the only place they feel safe and at ease. Unfortunately, these self-imposed restrictions and fears disrupt their lives and the lives of their family members. Erica M., a participant in one of our studies, talked about her eleven-year-old daughter, Lauren, who suffers from agoraphobia:

What If I Throw Up?

The other day our next-door neighbor, Margaret, came over with her little girl, Julie. She and Lauren are friends from school, and they play together in our yards all the time, so it's not like they're strangers at all. Margaret asked me if Lauren could go with them to get ice cream later in the day, and as soon as she asked me I felt the tension in my head flare up.

"I'm sure Lauren would love to go with you and Julie for ice cream. She loves ice cream! Let me talk to her a minute." I went over to Lauren and Julie and sat down on one of the swings. "Guess what? Julie's mom asked if you'd want to get ice cream with them later. How does that sound?"

Lauren answered with an enthusiastic, "Yes!"

"OK, I'll go tell Margaret she can pick you up when they're ready to go." I started walking over to Margaret to tell her, and before I got ten feet away, Lauren came running after me.

"Mommy! Wait! If I go with them I can't be back in time for Daddy to pick me up," Lauren said frantically, her eyebrows knit in a tight V-shape.

"Don't worry about that," I told her, "I can come pick you up at the ice cream stand, and we'll drive right over to Daddy's."

"That's not good," Lauren whined. "What if my stomach starts to hurt? What if I throw up? I'm going to throw up!"

That's always Lauren's out: she might throw up. I only remember her throwing up once in her life, after she drank a strawberry milkshake too fast. It was a scary thing for her, and now when her stomach hurts she's always afraid she's going to throw up again.

I could see that Margaret was listening to us sympathetically, so I said to Lauren, "How about we let Julie and her mom go ahead, and we can meet them there later if you feel like it? OK?" Lauren nodded cautiously, looking from me to Julie and Margaret.

Once they'd left, Lauren and I went inside the house, and she started crying. "I wanted to go with them! I wanted to go with them!" She said she'd ride her bike over to the ice cream stand, but I knew she wouldn't do it, even if I said she could go by herself. It's so frustrating to me to see her so upset, but there's nothing I can do to make it better. She's afraid to do new things or take a small risk, and then she gets mad at herself for being afraid.

I'm not going to let her stay in the house all the time. I don't want her to be too comfortable sitting in her room or watching TV all the time. It's too easy to just stay inside where it's safe.

PANIC DISORDER

Children and adolescents who suffer from panic disorder experience attacks of recurrent and unexpected terror ("panic attacks"). These attacks are the source of a great deal of discomfort and disruption in the lives of those suffering from them. Although panic disorder is rare in young children, it becomes more common among older children and adolescents.

The anxiety that agoraphobics experience when they feel trapped or exposed can become so intense that panic attacks occur. In fact, panic attacks almost always accompany agoraphobia, although nonagoraphobics also may be subject to them. Panic attacks may also feed the anxiety of agoraphobics, who may simply think about what would happen to them if they had a panic attack in a certain situation. Those who struggle with agoraphobia may also worry about being in a place where help may not be available if they do have an attack.

The panic attacks that constitute panic disorder are relatively short episodes of extreme anxiety, usually lasting between twenty to thirty minutes, typically reaching their peak within ten minutes. During a panic attack, the young person quickly and unexpectedly feels overwhelmed by terrifying mental and physical sensations that feed his anxiety. Some mental symptoms include a sense of impending death and doom and feelings of detachment. Those in the grip of a panic attack are usually unable to name the source of their terror, as they may feel very confused and have difficulty focusing their attention.

Therapists agree that in order to be classified as a panic attack, four or more of the following symptoms must develop abruptly and peak within ten minutes:

- Pounding heart, increased heart rate

- Sweating

- Trembling, shaking

- Chest pain or discomfort

- Nausea or abdominal discomfort

- Shortness of breath

- Choking sensation

- Dizziness or lightheadedness

- Feelings of unreality or detachment from self

- Fear of losing control or going crazy

- Fear of dying

- Numbness or tingling

Even though a child is not in the grip of a panic attack at a particular moment, his simply thinking that there is a strong possibility that he may have one without warning is enough to make that child highly anxious. This anticipatory response is caused by the child's expectation of having another attack and his focusing on that fear. His response may also include changing his lifestyle or behavior pattern to accommodate the possibility of another attack. It frequently results in a significant disruption of normal behavior. The difference between this anticipatory anxiety of children with panic disorder and generalized anxiety is that those who are prone to panic attacks can usually name the source of their anxiety, whereas those with generalized anxiety cannot. Alfred G., a participant in one of our studies, talked about his nine-year-old daughter, Mary, who suffers from panic attacks:

Hallway Panic

On her way to school, Mary starts to feel nervous and begins picking at her fingernails. As soon as she walks into her school's front door she feels her chest start to pound really fast and hard. With every step she takes, it seems like her chest is going to explode, and she starts really getting scared. Without warning, she can take only short shallow breaths, and drops her books to the floor. All she can do is stand still and plead with her watery eyes for someone to help her. A teacher down the hall notices her distress and rushes over to ask her what's wrong. Mary wants to tell him, but she can only whimper and sob. The teacher quickly escorts her to the nurse's office, where Mary is seated in a chair and comforted by the nurse and teacher. After a few minutes,

Mary is shaken up and scared, but she is breathing easier and her chest is beating much slower.

GENERALIZED ANXIETY DISORDER (GAD)

Children and adolescents with generalized anxiety disorder (GAD) have excessive or unrealistic worry in a variety of situations. They may spend more time than is appropriate paying attention to the details of such activities as homework or other normal tasks. Children with GAD may also experience any of the following physical symptoms:

- Restlessness

- Tiredness

- Difficulty concentrating

- Irritability

- Unusual muscle tension

- Sleep disturbance

One might say that a child with GAD "worries about worrying." That is, because he sees himself as an anxious person who cannot handle anxiety very well, he develops additional anticipatory anxiety when he is faced with even the possibility of being in an uncomfortable situation. In some cases, the child may refuse to attend school. If he experiences excessive worry along with even just one of the aforementioned physical symptoms and this occurs over a six-month period, the child is diagnosed as having GAD. It is not uncommon for children and adolescents with GAD to experience a panic attack at some point in their lives, in response to particularly anxious times.

The children who struggle with GAD are usually not difficult to spot, as their anxiousness seems to dominate a large portion of their lives. They may seem on edge most of the time, or they have extended periods of anxiousness that last for a few days and then fade, only to return days or weeks later. A source of great frustration for children with GAD and their parents is the difficulty in finding out exactly what is wrong. This frustration is understandable, as it is very difficult to fix something if you do not know where to look for the problem.

SEPARATION ANXIETY

Separation anxiety is particularly common among children and sometimes young adolescents. It occurs when the child is separated from familiar people and settings and involves a definite degree of discomfort or anxiety. If a child or adolescent experiences excessive anxiety (lasting at least four weeks) after routine separation from parents, other caregivers, or home or other familiar situations, he may be suffering from separation anxiety disorder.

Crying, clinging, or panic on separation are common reactions of small children who experience separation anxiety. The signs of separation anxiety disorder in older children and adolescents are unrealistic worry about potential harm to loved ones or fear they will not return home; reluctance to sleep alone; refusal to attend school; and physical symptoms, such as a stomachache or headache.

Sometimes it is difficult to identify fear of separation as the source of anxiety among older children or adolescents, because they are less likely to give off clear signals. However, instances of misbehavior and emotional displays occurring before, during, or after separation could be signs of distress. An important point to remember is that "symptoms" of separation anxiety don't always make sense to the outsider; one has to be observant and involved in order to pick up on the signals that older children and adolescents give off.

POSTTRAUMATIC STRESS DISORDER (PTSD)

Posttraumatic stress disorder (PTSD) is a very serious condition that has a wide range of dangerous implications. It is crucial that any child who is even suspected of having PTSD is provided professional assistance as soon as possible.

PTSD may occur after a child or adolescent has been exposed to a sudden or periodic traumatic event in which the threat of death or serious injury was presented to themselves or others. In addition, the child will have experienced intense fear, helplessness, or horror that serve to powerfully imprint the trauma in the child's mind.

The symptoms of PTSD in children and adolescents can present themselves in very complicated ways, but there are some things to watch for. Children may persistently reexperience the traumatic event as thoughts or feelings. They may show play behaviors that exhibit themes or aspects of the original traumatic event. Other symptoms include repeated bad dreams; intense avoidance of people, places, and things that serve as reminders of the trauma; inability to remember details of the trauma; physical or emotional detachment from others; narrow emotional range; sleep disorder; irritability; difficulty concentrating; and being easily startled. Symptoms usually appear within the first three months following the trauma, but it is possible that they may not surface until many months or years after the traumatic event.

PTSD can occur at any age, but identifying it among children and adolescents can be complicated. One reason for this complication is that most children and many adolescents have not yet fully developed an ability to express themselves effectively, so their thoughts and emotions about the trauma may be expressed only as agitated behavior. It is for this reason that caregivers should pay special attention to the possible signs of PTSD after a child has been exposed to any traumatic event. And as we mentioned earlier, PTSD always requires the intervention of a professional.

OBSESSIVE-COMPULSIVE DISORDER (OCD)

Children with OCD are troubled by persistent and recurring thoughts or "obsessions" that consume their attention for more than one hour a day and generally involve exaggerated anxiety or fears. These children feel compelled to perform repetitive behaviors, known as compulsions, in order to relieve or vent away anxiety and tensions caused by their obsessive thoughts.

Such compulsions as checking everything twice before leaving the house, returning to the house to see that there is no fire, and excessively washing, counting, praying, hoarding, and carrying out rituals are particularly common in young people with OCD. Usually it is not the behavior itself that is the problem but how often the child feels he must perform the behavior. The repetitiveness of the behavior provides comfort to the child, yet it creates terrible disruption in his day-to-day life. Marilyn T., also a participant in one of our studies, describes her twelve-year-old son, James, who suffers from OCD, this way:

Troubling Thoughts

James is a very bright boy, yet he has a great deal of trouble getting his schoolwork done. This is particularly frustrating to James, who very much wants to do well but who is constantly distracted by powerful and strange thoughts, such as counting how many times he blinks and how many steps it takes to get to the hallway. He feels compelled to avoid stepping on any floor tiles with dirt on them because he doesn't want to get germs on his feet. The possibility that germs could be on door handles or windows also forces him to avoid touching them unless he first uses a cloth (which he carries with him always) to clean them off. In fact, if he misplaces or forgets to bring a clean cloth with him, he feels a great deal of anxiety, feels paralyzed, and may get physically ill.

James realizes that his behavior doesn't make too much sense, and it frustrates him a lot that he can not overcome these powerful thoughts. Other classmates make fun of him and call him crazy. Increasingly, James has been staying home from school because he is embarrassed and upset with himself. His teachers are concerned about his absences and poor academic performance. They give James support, as much as they can, but they don't understand his behavior either.

We realize that reading about these disorders has probably caused you to feel some anxiety yourself. It's comparable to the "medical student syndrome." Many medical students suspect they have the symptoms of whatever malady they happen to be studying at the time. When reading about anxiety symptoms, parents may suspect that their child has many of the symptoms described in this chapter.

Nevertheless, knowing the distinctions among the eight types of anxiety disorders is necessary if you are to participate effectively in your child's rehabilitation. The good news is that almost all children who have one of these disorders can be helped a great deal. If you feel that your child may have the symptoms we described for agoraphobia, panic disorder, PTSD, or OCD, we strongly suggest that you consult a competent therapist or psychiatrist. You will be able to use many of the ideas in this book to help your child, but therapy should take place under professional supervision. For the other four problems, you can try using the activities recommended in this book on your own. If the problem does not resolve itself in a reasonable amount of time, you can still seek professional help.

Chapter Three

COPE Step One

Calming the Nervous System

Fight or Flee

The two hunters, an aging father and his young adult son, had been trotting along the ancient path since the sun had risen nearly four hours earlier. They had seen no targets worth the risk of losing a precious arrow. As they broke out of the thick woods onto the boulder-strewn plateau, the father stretched his hairy right arm above his head, the signal to pause for a rest. He and his son slowed to a stop at the base of a huge rock and slumped with their backs against it. They did not sit, as that would have left them too vulnerable to attack. Their feet, as tough as mammoth hide, were impervious to the shattered shale that surrounded them. Sweat trickled down their nearly nude bodies. They did not speak, as neither had anything to say.

For a few moments, their vigilant ears heard nothing but the wind. Then, faintly, the hiss of the breeze mingled with a different, pulse-quickening sound. The son was quicker to notice it—the telltale scratching of claw on rock. Elbowing his father, he motioned with his head to the top of the boulder and took a step away. As he did so, what he heard choked off the breath of both men—the deep bass rumble that could only come from the thick vocal chords of a saber-toothed tiger. Instantly, without making any attempt to investigate further, the son dropped his weapons and raced for the dubious haven of the forest. A heartbeat later, his father, slipping slightly on the loose gravel, bolted after him.

With branches grabbing at his face, the older man strained to catch sight of his son but could not discern which fork in the path the youth had taken. The father ran straight on, faster than he had ever run before, and after a few moments began to hope that the surprised tiger had lost him. Soon, however, the crash of his own feet in the underbrush merged with thudding drumbeats on the ground behind him. He dove on through the swirling brush, no longer looking for the path, his pace declining slightly as his terrified heart sped faster and faster but less and less efficiently.

Careening down another path not far away, his son heard too, and then, despite his fervently murmured prayer to the Mother, the dreaded moment of silence came. Inevitably, an inhuman scream and a series of unearthly snarls rent the silence. Finally, nothing reached his ears but the slap of his own thick soles against the packed dirt of the path.

In Chapter One, we mentioned the fight-or-flight reaction and how it helps us be on guard in stressful situations. It was this innate reaction of the nervous system that caused the hunters in our story to waste no time devising a plan for dealing with the saber-toothed tiger. The rush of adrenaline they experienced on first hearing the tiger's claws on the rock triggered more than twenty known physical reactions in their bodies. For example, their blood rushed to the large muscle groups of their bodies and away from their brains, and their breath became rapid and shallow. Some responses relate to specific tasks, such as the dilation of the pupils to improve focus and the raising of the hair on the upper back, which all animals use to make themselves appear somewhat larger. Most responses, however, have the effect of curbing thought and encouraging almost instant action.

There was some thought involved in the hunters' behavior. They quickly decided not to try to fight the tiger. They realized that weapons good for killing small animals would be of no help in their situation, so they dropped them. Having chosen not to fight, they had to run. Over millions of years, nature had instilled this hormonal lifesaver deep in their primitive brains. Although the fight-or-flight response did not save the older man, his son would probably have died too if he had paused to think of an innovative strategy for overwhelming the menacing beast.

It is ironic that even in modern times, with brains that have evolved tremendously, children (as well as adults) experience anxiety reactions that are born of primitive genetic traits. The fight-or-flight response fires up when your child perceives a threat, whether the threat is realistic or not. Today, however, children rarely confront such truly dangerous threats. Far more often, their fears and anxieties are provoked by concerns of a psychological or social nature. One example would be the terror many children feel when called on to give an oral report. They are in no more danger than when talking to a friend. Because they *perceive* themselves to be vulnerable, however, the ancient fight-or-flight reaction kicks in. Children may experience anger at the upturned faces of the audience, the "dragon with a thousand eyes," and simultaneously have a fervent desire to run off the stage and hide. But those are not considered appropriate responses. Children and adults alike need a third alternative, one that will allow them to use their heads coolly so that they may successfully tackle a given challenge.

An unfortunate side effect caused by the fight-or-fight response is increased vigilance. Vigilance means being in a constant state of watch—on the lookout for potential pitfalls. Being alert is usually an asset, but it can become a handicap when children exaggerate a present or anticipated danger. Vigilant children needlessly use energy in a constant surveillance of the environment. Their vigilance at that point is referred to as *hypervigilance*, a key symptom of the anxious child. A child who is highly anxious looks for things to worry about, such as a jungle gym that seems a bit too dangerous, the Halloween witch hiding in her closet, or the certainty that she is going to throw up if she is made to go to Sunday school.

The first step in combating anxiety is to help your child calm her nervous system so that she is not perpetually on alert. Calming is the focus of this chapter, corresponding to the first component of the COPE method described in Chapter One (C = calming the nervous system). Later in this chapter we will present a variety of techniques and activities that can reduce the harmful effects of stress through relaxation of hypervigilance. Subsequent chapters will focus on the three other components of the COPE method, which will ultimately provide you with a complete package of strategies and tactics to help alleviate your child's anxiety. First, however, let's look at how the human body deals with the stress we all experience; your understanding of this process will improve your ability to teach your child to relax.

THE ALARM REACTION

When your child experiences a crisis, she will initially have what is called an alarm reaction, and then eventually she adapts to the situation. In this section, we will explore the concepts of reaction and adaptation, which are crucial to understanding and reducing your child's stress.

When your child reacts with alarm to some situation, adrenal hormones pour into her bloodstream, where they are carried to all parts of her body like soldiers going to their battle stations. Their presence triggers physiological reactions that are often invisible to an adult's watchful eyes. Because of our experience of this phenomenon as psychologists, we have learned to place a hand on the inside of a child's wrist while we're talking. That way, we can take her pulse. You would be surprised how often a placid-looking child has a rapid heart rate, indicating an anxious state.

Often when anxious children become alarmed, their adrenal glands send out too many hormones, making these children all the more keyed up for the fight-or-flight response. This overload of hormones occurs because of mental errors (for instance, exaggerating the real threat), but it can also have physiological causes. The most common physiological complications are hyperadrenalism (overproduction of adrenal hormones), excessive ACTH (a hormone in the pituitary that can release too much adrenaline), hypoglycemia (the imbalance of proper blood sugar levels), and hyperventilation (breathing so rapidly that there is too much oxygen in the system).

Although this is a book about helping children help themselves, these physiological complications may require the expertise of a doctor. If you find that after having tried some of the methods described in this chapter the child is not having much success relaxing, then you should consider medical options, such as medication. This is also the case if your child regularly has an exaggerated alarm reaction, such as a high heart rate or trembling, that is not reduced significantly within about fifteen to twenty minutes after having experienced a crisis.

Human beings have an adaptation response built into their physiology that counteracts the alarm reaction; this response is known as the generalized adaptation syndrome. First recognized by Canadian physiologist Dr. Hans Selye, this adaptation response occurs in all people when the brain responds to the increased flow of hormone released as a result of the state of alarm. During this stage, your child's adrenal cortex secretes a stream of adrenaline, and the child may appear to be even stronger than before the initial shock.

However, this adaptation response is short lived. If your child continues to experience stress, her adaptational energies will begin to deplete. Eventually she will experience a stage of exhaustion, in which her physiological responses revert to their status before the alarm reaction. Over time, the pattern of reaction and adaptation wears on a child's physiological system much as scars mar a child's skin.

As a parent, you may recognize that the alarm state is characteristic of childhood. Children respond excessively to all kinds of stimuli and have not yet learned the basic ways to handle stress. Anxious children evidence this normal tendency in exaggerated cases. As children enter adolescence, they generally become better at handling the difficulties of everyday life, which reduces the intensity of some of their initial alarm reactions. Dr. Edward Hallowell, author of *Worry: Hope and Help for a Common Condition*, shares the following insights:

> Children worry. Sometimes adults forget how many worries fill even the happiest childhood. This is because childhood is a time of "firsts," of doing so many things for the first time. The first of anything is a little scary. The first day of school. The first sleepover. The first piano lesson. The first class in a foreign language. The first kiss. Exciting moments, but all potentially fraught with worry.
>
> In some ways, worry is what makes childhood so memorable. We remember how much we worried about such little things. Being popular. A pimple. Grades. Hitting a baseball. Being picked for . . . anything. . . .
>
> With any luck, children learn to get information to inform their worries and to help calculate their risks. They learn how to get comfortable with a certain amount of danger and when to pull back or go for help.

Regaining serenity and clear thinking is essential in refining self-control. Your child cannot achieve serenity if she does not recognize the presence of stress. Therefore, you should know what to look for when trying to help her identify it. There are a number of aids you can use to achieve this objective. In their excellent book, *How to Relax*, John Curtis and Richard Detert distinguish five categories of stressors: social (loud noise), psychological (self-doubt), psychosocial (death of a friend), biochemical (pollutants), and philosophical (loss of a sense of direction). Although there are many types of human reactions to stress, most of them result from one of these five stressors.

This chapter features an abundance of activities for you to do with your child. Some physical activities are primarily aimed at the subcortex of the brain, where the hormones will be affected and change the way your child is feeling: the physiological reaction ignites the calm that follows. Other activities are designed to affect the cortex and thus involve more active thinking. Still other activities are a combination, involving both areas of the brain. Whichever ones you think will be most appealing to your child, be sure to try one or more of each kind, because you can never tell in advance which one will prove most successful. Remember that you are the expert where your child is concerned. These activities are designed to be used, adapted, and tailored to fit the needs of your unique child.

USING PHYSICAL METHODS

Some children find that they can calm themselves best through physical means. This section offers a set of exercises that are quite different from each other. The more of them your child tries out, the more likely she is to find a good fit with her needs.

Abdominal Breath Control

One physical condition that frequently causes children (and adults) to experience intense anxiety is called *hyperventilation*, which is the medical term for rapid breathing. When a person breathes quickly and shallowly, using only the upper portion of the lungs, she experiences temporary symptoms, which can be very frightening for someone who doesn't understand what is happening. These are the symptoms:

- Dizziness and lightheadedness

- Strong feelings of apprehension

- Numbness in the lips

- Loss of coordination in the hands, feet, or both

- Tension or pain in the chest

- Rapid pulse

Every day, in hospital emergency rooms all over the country, people are brought in suffering from hyperventilation, in a state of terror because they fear they are dying. The problem is that they have too much oxygen in their systems and not enough carbon dioxide. Fortunately, holding their breath for a while or rebreathing exhaled air by holding a bag over their mouth can reverse the process.

Learning to breathe the right way, especially when distressed, calms us and allows us to think more clearly. Correct relaxation breathing involves inhalation, exhalation, and breath-holding maneuvers. The purpose of the breathing action described in the exercise that follows is to stretch your child's diaphragm at the base of the lungs. Nerves located in the diaphragm produce messages that set off the relaxation response in the brain. It will take some time, especially for younger children, to master this technique. It is best practiced just before going to bed, when it will help your child slip into a peaceful sleep, which will in turn reinforce the practice.

ACTIVITY

Abdominal Breathing Activity

Target Age: 5 to 17
Goal: To learn effective relaxation through correct breathing skills
Materials Needed: A supportive chair or exercise mat

Tell your child, "Your body is your friend! You can teach it to help you get over being afraid. You just need to know how. You can do this through breathing in a special way."

Ask your child to sit in a comfortable position but with her back straight and pressed into the chair for support. Some children may prefer to lie down on a foam mat or pad. Loose clothing is a good idea. With a younger child, take her pulse rate; have adolescents do it themselves. To find the number of heartbeats per minute, press your fingers into the side of your child's neck, count the beats for fifteen seconds, and then multiply that number by four to arrive at the number of beats per minute.

Have your child inhale slowly to a count of five, then slowly exhale. After she has practiced several times, ask your child to place her hand on her belly and to make her hand move out as she breathes deeply into her abdomen. Say, "Make your tummy stick out as though it had a watermelon in it." Tell her to breathe in slowly while counting in her head for four seconds ("one Mississippi, two . . ."), and up to six seconds for teens. Your child should breathe out the same way and then hold her breath for four seconds. Repeating this sequence creates the maximum relaxation. Breathing must be done slowly—rapid breathing can produce hyperventilation, which can raise anxiety levels.

If your child finds the method we have described hard to do, have her "huff and puff" as fast as she can, then try to do exactly the opposite. Remind the child to keep her shoulders low and loose.

The purpose of this rapid breathing technique is to stretch your child's diaphragm at the base of the lungs. Nerves located in the diaphragm produce messages that set off the relaxation response in the brain. It will take some time, especially for younger children, to master the technique. It is best practiced just before going to bed, when it will help your child slip into a peaceful sleep, which will in turn reinforce the practice.

Anxious children often worry that they will not be able to get enough air, that they're going to faint or suffocate. Discuss this with your child and reassure her that even if she feels the room is stuffy, her throat feels as though it is closing, and her legs get wobbly, there still will be enough air. Tell your child, "Don't worry, your breathing will be good enough so that you will be OK, even if you become very frightened."

All of us can remember times when our anxiety level has gone through the roof. Lisa recalls a time when her breathing method helped her deal with terror.

Panic in the Dentist's Chair (LF)

As early as when I was two years old, I experienced problems with my teeth that required a dentist's attention. The feeling of my sweaty hands gripping the arms of the dentist's chair, the sterile smell of the office, the bright light shining down into my eyes, and the piercing sound of the drill are memories that can still raise goosebumps. During my early school years, I had baby teeth pulled and cavities filled, and I wound up dreading the seemingly monstrous needle that would inject the novocaine into my oral nerves. My heart would beat so fast and hard in my chest that I could hear it in my ears.

When I was told that I would need to have my wisdom teeth pulled at age sixteen, all of the fear came creeping back. Because I had no desire to experience the procedure, my parents and I opted for a combination of local anesthesia and laughing gas. Shortly after the doctor placed the mask over my mouth and told me to breathe in and out, the sounds in the room became slightly metallic. I remember thinking, "Am I counting backwards in my head, or can they all hear me?" I wasn't sure, but I thought it was pretty hilarious.

From time to time Dr. P. asked me how I was doing. At one point he asked me, "Are you *sure* you're OK?" I started to think, "Maybe something's wrong. Maybe I'm *not* OK." I felt and heard my heart beating faster, and then I realized that I was unintentionally holding my breath because I was feeling tense with worry. I made a conscious effort to "breathe in, two, three, four, five . . . exhale, two, three, four, five." I did this over and over again and drifted off into sleep.

When I woke up, I was in the recovery room. Everything seemed extremely white and bright. I still felt a little woozy. When the doctor came in for a brief follow-up, he told me that everything looked fine. He asked me what I had done during the surgery to calm down. I wasn't sure what he was talking about, but my mother later told me that I had been a "bleeder," and at one point I was bleeding quite a bit from an incision the surgeon had made. All of a sudden, however, the doctor noticed that the bleeding slowed, then stopped completely, and I fell asleep.

Although I don't remember the walk from the recovery room to the elevator, the elevator ride to the garage, or much of the car ride home, I do clearly remember breathing rhythmically during the surgery. It was something that I had to tell myself to do—it did not just "happen." As a result, I have used that breathing technique many times since, whenever I feel nervous. This requires that I am calm enough to recognize that, yes, I am feeling scared about something, and yes, I can do something about it, and the results are worth the effort.

Sensory Awareness

In the everyday world, children are constantly bombarded by stimuli from the environment: traffic, machines, the media, and so on. It is no wonder children lose track of their inner environment—their heart and breathing rates; tension in their muscles, ligaments, and tendons; pain in their joints, colon, and vessels—as they grow up. Sensory awareness is a way for your child to discover what these inner stimuli are and how they are affecting her. As she becomes aware of these stimuli, you can work with your child to adapt procedures for alleviating stress and strain. In this manner your child will become better able to deal with problems presented by the outer world.

ACTIVITY

◎ 3B ◎

Getting to Know Your Orange!

Target Age: 5 to 10
Goal: To focus on sensory awareness and recognize abilities to use all five senses
Materials Needed: Three or four oranges, one large paper bag

Give your child an orange and tell her to "get to know it." Have her study her orange for size, bumps, dents, and any other noticeable traits. Then write your child's name on her orange with a felt-tipped pen and place all the oranges in the large bag. Ask your child to reach in the bag and try to find her orange, without being allowed to look. Amazingly, most of the time a child can find her orange. (At least we have found this to be so for children five and older.)

Return your child's orange to the bag. Next, ask her to tell you how she recognized her orange. Then ask her to suggest other objects that could be used for the game and to tell you what identifying characteristics she would look for. Finally, see how many attributes she can think of to identify various objects: taste, use, meaning, historical origin, "bounceability," "squashability," and so on.

Venting Emotions

Sometimes your child merely needs to vent, even if it seems silly to do so. Punching pillows and stuffed animals, drawing a picture of a bully or a rival and privately stamping her foot on it, writing notes or letters to a person that are never sent . . . each can be a way to help a child cool off.

Although venting tension by harming others is unacceptable, punishing an object such as a pillow that can stand for the upsetting situation can be a healthy outlet for your child.

ACTIVITY

 3C

Make a Personal Punching Pillow

Target Age: 5 to 10
Goal: To release tension in a nonthreatening activity
Materials Needed: Paper, crayons or markers, a safety pin, and a pillow or old cushion

Have your child draw a picture of a stressful situation or person. If your child is having trouble thinking of what or who to draw, you might suggest, "Draw me a picture of what is making you scared [or angry]." When she is finished, help her pin the drawing to the pillow or cushion and let her hit it as much as is necessary to express the pent-up feelings. Alternatives are stamping on the picture, crushing it into a ball, or scribbling on it.

Adaptation for Older Children: Your child could sculpt figures from soap or clay, or represent the situation with a miniature stage setting made from popsicle sticks or pipe cleaners.

Each of these activities can release tension and allow your child to express feelings that are sometimes difficult to talk about. Explain to your child that her actions are meant to help her release her feelings so that she can think about things in a more calm and rational manner. Once the pent-up energy is released, you will be surprised at how much easier it is to talk with her about the anxiety-provoking situation or person.

It is important to note that in some cases, mildly violent activities increase, rather than decrease, children's anxiety. You will know best what type of venting will work well with your child's personality. Less physical alternatives for children include talking to the picture ("I'm not afraid of you!") or generating a list of adjectives describing the person or situation. Children can also vent tensions by such neutral actions as squeezing a tennis ball (or a ball of clay or dough, or a spring-type hand exerciser) or singing at the top of their lungs.

Aerobic Exercise

Aerobic exercise is any exercise that involves continuous rhythmic movement of the large muscles. It should be vigorous enough for your child to reach her target heart rate (as described in the next activity). For most children, this kind of exercise needs to be done at least four times a week for at least thirty minutes, although for beginners a shorter duration is advised. For most children, brisk walking will also achieve this goal.

Your child will derive at least three benefits from aerobic exercise:

- A good workout loosens her muscles and ligaments, thus reducing existing tensions.

- Well-toned muscles are less likely to tense up and become painful, even when the child's mind is stressed.

- It will dispel the common fear that if she becomes very afraid, her heart will beat so fast it will explode or cause her to faint. If she learns to take her pulse during an "anxiety attack," she will find that it is almost always lower than during aerobic exercise.

ACTIVITY

 **3D**

Know Your Own Heart Rate

Target Age: 5 to 17
Goal: To be introduced to her heart rate and foster awareness of her ability to both raise and lower it
Materials Needed: Wristwatch or clock with a second hand

To calculate your child's target heart rate (THR), subtract her age from 220, then multiply the result by .7 and .85. The two numbers yield the range within which your child's heart rate should fall. When her pulse is taken within five seconds of stopping exercise, her pulse should be somewhere between these two numbers. For example, if your child is ten, calculate her THR range as follows:

$220 - 10 = 210$
$210 \times .7 = 147$
$210 \times .85 = 179$
Thus her THR is between 147 and 179.

Take your child's pulse by pressing two fingers into her carotid artery (at the side of the neck) for twenty seconds, then multiply by three. Most children's pulses are between 60 and 80 beats per minute; aerobic exercise usually brings it up to between 140 and 180.

Have your child do some aerobic activity for twenty to thirty minutes and take her pulse again. Share the differences with your child, allowing her to see that her pulse rate is significantly higher than it was before she did the aerobic activity. She may be surprised at the difference, and you can remind her that she can lower her rate by taking deep breaths. Take her pulse after a cool-down period as a nice way to make a final comparison between pulse rates before, during, and after aerobic activity.

Supportive Surfaces

Supportive surfaces are those that support us when we are standing, sitting, or lying down. Sometimes a child feels anxious because she is being aggravated in ways she may not consciously perceive. For example, some children feel more comfortable sitting in a chair that has armrests and is more confining, whereas other children may find such restriction of movement uncomfortable. It may help you relate to the idea of supportive surfaces to think about sleeping on a mattress. Some people prefer a firm mattress, and others cannot sleep comfortably unless their mattress is as soft as a featherbed.

Which would you rather sit on: a lumpy old couch, a straight-backed chair, a bucket car seat, or a plush recliner? As you can see, these supportive surfaces have been arranged in order, from less to more comfortable support. In this case, the principal area being supported is the lower back. When not exercised regularly, the back muscles get weak, and children cannot sit still without becoming tense and irritable. Sitting without firm support of the lordosis (the curved area in the lower back) will soon produce tension, which quickly transfers into a negative mental attitude. The point is that keeping your child in a relaxed frame of mind and body depends to a large extent on how supportive the surfaces are on which she rests. This does not apply only to sitting. When long periods of standing are required, make sure some kind of pressure-absorbent pad is available on the floor.

Those Lumpy Old Camp Chairs (JD)

For thirteen years I was director of an overnight camp for about sixty youngsters ranging in age from six to sixteen, many of them with emotional problems. There wasn't much money for expenses, so we equipped the place with old chairs and sofas donated by parents. All of this furniture was on its last legs, ragged and lumpy, with an occasional spring popping through.

After a half-hour or so of sitting on this furniture, I noticed that many of the campers were fidgeting and changing positions. I found myself getting more tense from sitting on the furniture, too, and had to get up and walk around after a while to relieve the tension.

For some children, the tension also increased their anxiety levels. This did not happen when they were lying around on the ground, as they often did in good weather. We learned that when the children were sitting on bad furniture, their physical discomfort made them more likely to express fears about activities that required a little risk taking.

Massage

Psychologist Tiffany Field studied the use of massage to treat the victims of Hurricane Andrew, many of whom were children suffering from PTSD. She found that after a month of massage therapy (two times per week) the children's depression and anxiety decreased and their self-image improved.

There is a lot of other evidence that massage can help reduce anxiety, especially if you encourage your child to try to remember the feeling at the end of a massage and bring that feeling to mind when under stress. Massage can be expensive, but it might be covered under medical insurance if GAD is diagnosed. Inexpensive massage can also be obtained at schools that teach it. There are also many books and articles (see the Annotated Bibliography) and local classes that teach the techniques of massage for children. You could also massage your child without seeking out a practitioner. Massage is a great activity for you and your child; touch and massage are natural ways of communicating and can form the basis for a secure and trusting relationship between you. It involves spending time together and getting to know each other better in a completely relaxed setting.

Before starting this activity, be sure to choose a time when you and your child won't be interrupted. Also, it is better to schedule this time with your child when there is no conflicting television program your child would rather be watching or some social event she would rather be attending. Your child needs to be with you mentally as well as physically, for this is the best way to truly relax.

ACTIVITY

Massage Therapy

Target Age: 5 to 17
Goal: To relax muscles and recognize the sensation of relaxation, which can be remembered and recreated on future occasions
Materials Needed: Exercise mat or soft blanket, relaxing music, and candles

Have your child lie on the floor, on top of a thin pad or soft blanket. Use your imagination to create a special atmosphere where your child is able to let go of tensions: put on some soft music or other soothing sounds; dim the lights or light an aromatic candle.

There is no right or wrong sequence to giving your child a massage. Some people like to focus on one particular part of the body, such as the back or shoulders; others begin at the head and work their way down to their child's toes. Sometimes focusing on one area for a longer period of time is more rewarding, and many people agree that having their feet massaged feels best of all. You and your child can figure out what feels the most relaxing. Be sure to pay attention to both verbal and nonverbal cues that your child gives you.

When you are finished giving your child a massage, switch places if you want to and let your child take a turn as the masseuse if she feels comfortable doing so. You may find that she isn't able to give you a massage—she may fall asleep!

Biofeedback

Closely aligned to sensory awareness, biofeedback involves measuring some biological trait such as changes in blood pressure, heart rate, skin temperature, amount of sweat, or galvanic skin response (GSR) on the hands. Biofeedback is information about one of these traits that is continuously reported to the person being measured. Research has shown that when people are aware of their scores on these biological indicators, especially when they are striving to relax, they are able to reduce their scores and thus their stress level. GSR is perhaps the best test, but until recently it could only be measured by an expensive electronic meter. Now there are cheaper and much more convenient measures that you can use, such as a plastic card that changes colors in your hand depending on how tense you are, or even an inexpensive "mood" ring.

If you are interested in finding more information about GSR and biofeedback, there are several ways you can proceed. First, the Internet is a rich source of information about biofeedback and various mechanisms that are designed to provide you with accurate readings of stress levels. Typing in such keywords as *biofeedback, galvanic skin response*, and *stress* will produce a plethora of websites. Another option is to visit a local health food or nutrition store. Many of these stores either stock inexpensive GSR devices or can refer you to an appropriate supplier. Finally, your physician or your child's pediatrician is an excellent source of information. Doctors are generally familiar with the concept of stress related to heart rate or cholesterol, and they will be able to provide immediate feedback in the form of a blood pressure reading or simply by placing a stethoscope against your child's chest. Listening to the beats, she can attempt to slow them while she listens through the stethoscope.

The actual process of biofeedback appears to take place in the unconscious. It is unknown why some people are better at using biofeedback than others. However, almost everyone experiences success if they practice with biofeedback techniques. More important, they become better able to calm themselves even when they are not receiving the biological information.

ACTIVITY

◎ 3F ◎

Body Sense

Target Age: 10 to 15
Goal: To release tensions through the biofeedback technique
Materials Needed: Stethoscope or biofeedback machine (both optional)

Once you've learned to use the equipment, spend as many sessions as is reasonable practicing with your child in the use of biofeedback to calm the nervous system. Keep a chart of the data produced by the equipment so that your child can see the progress she is making. There is no special technique involved; just getting the feedback seems to help the brain learn to relax itself and the rest of the body. If you cannot obtain the equipment, take your child's pulse while she tries to relax, and report the data to her regularly; this technique will work almost as well.

USING MENTAL METHODS

For some children, the physical techniques presented in the previous section work best. However, there are many for whom mental methods are more effective. Although some of the strategies in this section have a physical component, they rely mainly on mental techniques for their calming effect.

Paradoxical Thinking

Perhaps the most curious method for calming the nervous system is paradoxical thinking. This technique asks your child to give up trying to avoid anxious thoughts and instead try to get the frightening thoughts to come. That is, the child tries hard to make herself even more upset by imagining "the worst." Then the paradox comes into play: when children try to frighten themselves, doing so usually has the opposite effect of calming them down. This phenomenon probably occurs because the method gives children a feeling of being in control of their thoughts, which in turn helps them feel more in control of their actions.

ACTIVITY

3G

Can You Top This?

Target Age: 5 to 10
Goal: To stimulate creative and unusual thinking
Materials Needed: None

When your child is feeling anxious, talk to her to try to determine the focus of her anxiety. Suggest that she explain to you the specifics of her concern. In the process of talking about what is bothering her, she may begin to feel frightened. When her anxiety begins to rise, ask her to tell you how the situation could be worse, so that she would feel even more afraid. Then it is your turn to imagine an even more scary or uncomfortable set of circumstances and to describe them to your child. For example, your child may say she is afraid of a scary witch. You can then describe a witch with big, warty hands and worms for hair. Your child may then counter with a witch who breathes fire and smells like rotten eggs, who flies on a vacuum cleaner. The hypothetical situations will continue to grow in both absurdity and hilarity, and eventually your child will realize that things are not as bad as they seem. In this contest to see who can visualize the worst-case scenario, believe it or not, both people usually wind up laughing!

Adaptation for Older Children: Try having your child draw a picture of what she is scared of, then you and she alternate adding something to the picture. Eventually you will have a messy, silly drawing that will help her see how seemingly scary things can be turned into harmless, humorous things.

Scale Those Fears

In the next activity, creating a fear scale allows your child to chart fearful episodes. Performing the self-analysis that this task requires will help calm her. Over time, this process tends to reduce the severity of the episodes. Even more important, it will help your child establish a documented pattern that will be invaluable in creating imaginative plans for handling frightening situations in the future (more on this in Chapter Six).

ACTIVITY

3H

Scale Those Fears!

Target Age: 10 to 17
Goal: To interrupt anxious obsessions and reduce their severity
Materials Needed: Index cards, pen or pencil

Ask your child to describe the situation in which she felt the most panic. Ask her to describe another one that was equally bad. Assign a score of 10 to incidents like that. Now ask her to imagine herself to be completely relaxed. That's level 1. Finally, ask her to think of times when she has felt halfway between these two extremes. Those are level 5 anxieties.

Make up some three-by-five cards with the following headings written atop columns across the five-inch side: date, anxiety level number, feelings, thoughts. Any time your child experiences anxiety above level 3, as soon as possible she should find a private place and fill out a line (or more) on the card. If your child is in the beginning writing stages, she can dictate her feelings for you to write on the cards.

Adaptation for Younger Children: Ask your child to pick an appealing scene from one of her favorite books. Then have her pick a scene that she finds frightening. Continue picking scenes of each kind until she has an array of scenes that she can rank from high to low. Then discuss with her why she made her choices. As she scales the scenes, you can help her to gain perspective on what situations make her anxious.

Visualization

The ability to visualize, which may include mental notions of taste and touch as well as sight, is truly vital to anxiety control. The ability to imagine physical conditions and desired outcomes plays a role in a number of the techniques we are recommending in this book.

Our research has found that inner-city children are less skilled in this area than suburban youngsters. In fact, inner-city children are less likely to have been asked to imagine things in general—imagination is not a priority when there are more urgent needs that must be met. Relaxation in general and control of anxiety in particular demand good visualizing skills, and the only way to get them is through practice.

In the list that follows are some images we have used in our research on the visualization abilities of students. You may want to try these yourself or with your child:

- Can you see your own name clearly in your mind?
- Can you spell it backwards?
- Can you spell "bus stop" backwards with your eyes closed?
- Can you picture what an elephant looks like?
- What kind of ears does it have?
- How many notches does it have on its trunk?

ACTIVITY

Pretty Pictures in Your Mind

Target Age: 10 to 17
Goal: To develop increased visual ability
Materials Needed: Index cards, pen or pencil

First, ask your child to close her eyes and imagine as many as seven scenes that she finds particularly tranquil. Next, request that she write a phrase describing each scene on an index card and arrange the cards in descending order in terms of their degree of tranquility. With a younger child, have her dictate her ideas to you, or else let her choose scenes from pictures in magazines that appeal to her. Your child's list may look like this:

1. Waves on shore
2. Field of wheat or corn
3. Glowing embers in a fireplace
4. Wildflower meadow
5. Sleeping child in a crib
6. Botanical garden
7. Neighborhood park

Choose one of the scenes and ask your child to describe it in greater detail. Go through the list of scenes until she has described each one. Suggest to your child that she memorize the list and practice visualizing each scene. Later when she feels anxious, she can visualize each place on the list sequentially, and each step will help her calm down. Her list also helps you understand tranquility from her point of view; use her descriptions as a vocabulary to draw from as you're trying to understand her.

Adaptation for Younger Children: Use illustrations from children's books in a manner similar to that described in Activity 3H.

Self-Hypnosis

Visualization can be carried one step further. Using it in what we call self-hypnosis magnifies its effect. In teaching urban middle school students to relax when under stress—a condition with which most of them are familiar—we taught them to take themselves to an imaginary place where they would be able to control their stress levels completely within their own minds. They came to believe that when they went to this magical location, they were "under," and they could deal with their surroundings with more tranquility. There are a number of other techniques that work equally well.

ACTIVITY

 3J

Going Under

Target Age: 5 to 17
Goal: To encourage a state of relaxation and learn how to recreate it in the future
Materials Needed: None

Begin by asking your child to count backwards, beginning with number seven and ending with number one. As she begins with "seven," have her picture a relaxing scene. (It could be one of the scenes from Activity 3I.) Also tell her to press the tip of her right thumb against the tips of the middle two fingers of her right hand. This position of the fingers represents "completion of the circuit" of the relaxation cycle. With each number she says, have her picture a relaxing scene in her mind.

Each time your child pictures a different scene, she reinforces the cycle of relaxation. The more your child practices this technique, the less time it will take to calm her nervous system (which is true for *all* relaxation techniques). Soon your child will achieve tranquility merely by counting backward from seven to one while touching her thumb and fingers together.

Distraction

When the child's mind begins to race with an onslaught of thoughts that seem to have a will of their own, and the disturbing ideas are so persistent that your child cannot block them despite her best efforts, she should use some sort of distraction. Distractions can also calm the nervous system so that she can find a creative solution to her difficulty. Distractions are mental operations, but they are typically "mindless"; that is, their goal is to engage the mind in something so simple and routinized that the more destructive thoughts are prevented. Therefore, the sooner in a stressful situation your child implements distraction exercises, the more effective they are likely to be.

ACTIVITY

3K

Count Those Sheep

Target Age: 5 to 10
Goal: To use repetition as a means of relaxing and focusing on something other than anxiety-provoking situations
Materials Needed: None

Sometimes a repetitive activity proves effective. Everyone is familiar with the practice of counting sheep to become sleepy. Counting anything can help to break the anxiety cycle. Suppose you and your child are waiting at the airport for your flight to be called, and her fear level starts to rise. You notice the signs of stress even before she says anything. "Are you starting to feel frightened?" you ask.

"I guess I am," she replies.

"Let's try this," you say. "Let's both count all the tiles on the ceiling of this room and see if we get the same number. Take your time and do it as carefully as you can, and I will, too." While counting, keep glancing to see if she continues to be engaged in the task. If she stops, point out that she was successful in doing it for a while, and suggest that the two of you begin again. This exercise is particularly helpful for young children.

Adaptation for Older Children: You and your child can brainstorm many other distraction techniques, such as describing pleasant experiences. Write these ideas on cards with a few key words describing them printed on it. Then, when an anxiety-producing situation occurs, bring out the deck of cards and try the exercises. In time, just a list of the key words will suffice.

ACTIVITY

"Ouch!"

Target Age: 10 to 17
Goal: To use sensory experience to stifle negative thoughts
Materials Needed: Rubber bands

Ask your child to wear a rubber band around her wrist. When she feels overwhelmed by catastrophic thoughts, she should snap it against the inside of her wrist. Most children find that this soon eliminates their obsessive thinking, because their minds quickly associate the anxious thoughts with the uncomfortable sting, and try to avoid it.

As with the exercise on venting emotions presented earlier in this chapter, you need to be careful that this activity does not itself provoke anxiety. A less painful alternative might be to do some boring task such as turning the hands of a watch twelve hours forward or reciting a long dull poem. If the child forces herself to perform a boring activity each time the catastrophic thought occurs, a negative association will be formed that will come to suppress the thought.

Humor

A good laugh can also serve as a distracting device. Laughter actually produces a surge of endorphins, which are hormones that cause a sense of pleasure and well-being. Endorphin flow can have a calming effect for hours. There are many studies of the use of humor to relieve stress and lessen anxious behaviors such as hypervigilance.

The next activity is one in which the whole family can participate—the more people, the better!

ACTIVITY

3M

Ha!

Target Age: 5 to 17
Goal: To use laughter as a tension reliever
Materials Needed: A rug or a blanket

On the rug or on top of a blanket, have each person lie down on her back with her head resting on the stomach of another person, so that, in effect, the group forms a chain of people, head on stomach, head on stomach, and so on. The group can form a line or a circle, depending on how people are more comfortable and the size of the room.

Designate one person to begin. Have that person say the word "Ha!" loudly and boisterously, releasing the sound from the diaphragm. The head of the person whose head is on the speaker's stomach will bounce up and down as the speaker exhales the word "Ha!" The next person in line says "Ha!" followed by the next person, and the next, until everyone has said it, and the pattern continues until inevitably everyone is laughing. It is very hard not to laugh when your head is bouncing up and down, and anxious thoughts have a way of disappearing.

COMBINING PHYSICAL AND MENTAL METHODS

Some of the most effective relaxation techniques are those that combine physical and mental elements. The combination of thoughts and physiological responses appears to produce a reinforcement, each of the other, resulting in a strong calming effect. In this section, we explain how several of these methods work.

Autogenic Training

Earlier in this chapter, we discussed the benefits of having a relaxed body, in particular the benefit of having a relaxed mind in order to think clearly. Autogenic training, which means using mental images to bring about physiological states, has been researched extensively, and studies have found it to have many beneficial effects, such as strengthening the immune system and freeing creativity. It involves using both mind and body awareness to switch off the fight-or-flight response and replace it with a rest and relaxation response. Children can learn to recognize and summon the feelings striven for by autogenic training, that is, by what is called passive concentration. This means being conscious of their surroundings, but from a distance.

Autogenic training benefits your child by helping her

- Relieve headaches
- Reduce blood pressure and heart rate
- Enhance creativity, especially when your child is experiencing some sort of "mental block"
- Reduce episodes of insomnia
- Prevent hyperventilation attacks
- Alleviate backaches
- Control panic attacks
- Alleviate symptoms of anxiety, which include nausea, vomiting, diarrhea, constipation, short temper, and inability to get along with others
- Reduce overall stress and achieve greater inner peace and emotional balance

There are many variations of autogenic training; we describe the activity we like best. Stretching both emotionally and physically, your child will achieve a relaxed mind that allows her to think clearly about ways to manage her anxiety. This version has been taught to many individuals and groups. It is written for older children and teens; you will need to simplify the script for younger children. You may wish to tape-record this script so that your child can practice it on her own.

ACTIVITY

 3N

The Yogic Sponge

Target Age: 5 to 17
Goal: To reach a deep state of relaxation and emotional serenity
Materials Needed: Exercise mat, thick blanket, or rug

Have your child begin with a series of stretching exercises (a few minutes of virtually any easy stretches). Next, suggest to your child that she lie down on a firm but cushioned surface. Read this script in a soft, soothing voice.

"Put your hands beside you with your palms down, then let them turn up by themselves naturally. Let your feet spread apart a little bit. Get stretched out and try to get yourself in a nice relaxed position. The idea is to go on a mental trip. Instead of going on a trip away from home, you're going into the deepest part of yourself, your own personal home. This is a time specifically just for you, nobody else. You're going to be thinking only about getting yourself into position, so that you can do some really good relaxing. [Pause]

"Concentrate on your feet, especially your toes. Wiggle them around a little bit. Tense your feet up a little bit if you want to, pull them toward you, and then just let them go. Let them just relax completely. That's really good. [Pause]

"Now let this feeling of relaxation spread up into your ankles, shinbones, up to your knees. You may want to straighten your legs out and bend them just a little bit. Make sure the tightness is out of your knees, then let this mellow feeling move up your thighs. Your muscles are letting go, and now your legs are starting to become very, very heavy. They are pressing down against the rug and maybe almost through the rug. It feels wonderful to just lie there and sink deeper into this state of serenity. [Pause]

"This feeling now is beginning to spread up into your hips and your lower abdomen, up into your stomach. It is beginning now to filter into your chest. Notice that as you start to relax, your breathing now becomes slower. In fact, you can take a deep breath, hold it for a while, and let it go. Try it now—I'll count so that you can tell how long to do each of these three tasks.

First let all your breath out, *all* your breath. Now you're going to inhale, one, two, three, four, five, six, seven, eight, hold it two, three, four, five, six, seven, eight, let it out, two, three, four, five, six, seven, eight. As you practice this, you're going to become just like a sponge, just lying there soaking things up. You want to get your breathing to start to become slower and slower and deeper and deeper. Not just in your chest, but down in your belly. [Pause]

"Now let the feeling spread into your shoulders. Scrunch your shoulders up a little bit, wiggle them around, and make sure that they really let go. Let them 'fall' into the floor, so that your entire body now feels very, very heavy. [Pause]

"This feeling of heaviness is starting to move through your shoulders into your upper arms, down through your elbows, and now it's flowing down into your forearms. Your arms are becoming very heavy. [Pause]

"This feeling is now going into your palms, the backs of your hands, slowly going out through your fingers and your thumbs, a feeling of heaviness and deep relaxation. [Pause] Now return back up through your shoulders and into your neck. [Pause]

"Let this feeling come up through your chin, up through the back of your head and into your face. Your mouth is probably a little bit open, because you're doing nice deep breathing in through your nose and out through your mouth, feeling it up through your nose and cheekbones, even your ears. Concentrate on total, total relaxation. [Pause]

"Next check your eyes and make sure that they're just barely closed. Let this feeling of relaxation go up now through your forehead. It's a very lovely heavy feeling. The feeling is now up through your scalp, and you're extremely relaxed. [Pause]

"Your whole body feels like a big, big heavy rock. It's very pleasant. You have no responsibilities except to make yourself relax. Now I would like you to concentrate on that part of your face that is directly between your eyes and the top of your nose. Imagine that a magical golden fluid is starting to pour into your head through this special opening in the center of your forehead, down right between your eyes. You feel a golden yellow liquid, like honey, a warm relaxing fluid, just tremendously relaxing as it moves into your head now and fills your head and down through your neck. [Pause]

"You feel it flowing down inside, down through your shoulders and your arms, through your hands. It gives you total peace. Now it's starting to flow to fill your entire upper body, starting to flow into your legs. Slowly but surely you feel this warm, relaxing sensation surge down through you, down through your knees, down through your shins and your calves, total relaxation and a sense of safety and peace. Total peace floods through you and now down through your ankles into your feet, all the way through your feet down to your toes. And now your entire body is filled with this serene, warm, golden fluid. [Pause, then speak in a slightly softer voice.]

"Instead of feeling heavy, now, you notice that you've developed a feeling of lightness, as though you're floating. You're completely relaxed. You're thinking of nothing but the warm, very comfortable feeling that you're getting from this. And you're sinking down into it. You're letting yourself just be filled with this. You hear my voice very well, but it seems like it's from far away. And you find yourself drifting farther and farther away. You're thinking of nothing, nothing at all, but the peace that's there. You may want to picture a scene, like looking at the ocean or some other beautiful place. You do not feel sleepy, you do not feel tired at all, you feel just very, very comfortable, very safe, at peace. [Pause]

"You're filled with peacefulness, you're filled with the wonderful sense of freedom. Nothing's bothering you at all. You're at peace. You are now down in a very special, safe place, deep inside yourself, completely relaxed and completely safe. [Pause]

"All right, now start to think about coming back up to the surface again. You feel yourself sort of floating back up. You have become so light and free that you're actually floating. As you start to reenter the 'outside world,' you may want to just wiggle a finger. Do it slowly, at your own pace. Slowly come back. Move your feet around a little bit if you want to. As you feel ready to do it, open your eyes. Eventually you may want to get up on one elbow. [Pause]

"Gradually get yourself up to a sitting position. And get ready now, because I'm going to turn the light back on. Now think back.

Do you feel calmer? Happier? More mentally alert? Would you like to do this again sometime?"

Meditation

One of the simplest techniques available to us is what Dr. Herbert Benson calls inducing the "relaxation response." Dr. Benson defines the relaxation response as "the inborn capacity of the body to enter a special state characterized by lowered heart rate, decreased rate of breathing, lowered blood pressure, slower brain waves, and an overall reduction of the speed of metabolism." One of the benefits of this response is your child's ability to offset the uncomfortable feelings of stress. The method Benson describes works by interfering with what he calls worry cycles. Anxious children develop worry cycles when they replay, over and over again, almost involuntarily, the same anxieties or uncreative, health-impairing thoughts.

In his book *The Relaxation Response*, Dr. Benson recommends four steps to activate the relaxation response:

1. Find a quiet environment.
2. Consciously relax the body's muscles.
3. Focus for ten to twenty minutes on a mental stimulus called a mantra, such as the word *one* or a brief prayer.
4. Assume a passive attitude toward intrusive thoughts, such as the question, "Why am I doing this silly exercise?" (That is, when such thoughts intrude, don't fight them but simply allow them to go on freely. Allow yourself to feel as though you are floating above it all, merely observing your thoughts without acting on them.)

Transcendental meditation is based on the repetition of a mantra—any word or phrase that is particularly appropriate or pleasing to your child's personality. Any word or phrase will do—it is the repetition that matters, and there are many benefits. Monks in the Himalayas, for example, are able to achieve amazing feats of self-control (drastically reduced heart rate, increased body temperature, and the like) through meditation and chanting. If the child uses some phrase or prayer, some mantra that expresses her own belief system in some way that is powerful to her, she will attain even better results with the method.

ACTIVITY

Evoking Benson's "Relaxation Response"

Target Age: 10 to 17
Goal: To foster a relaxation technique that can be used independently, in any environment
Materials Needed: None

Use the following steps to achieve the relaxation response:

1. Help your child select a brief phrase or word that reflects her basic values or holds some particular meaning for her.
2. Instruct your child to choose a comfortable position on the rug (lying down, sitting cross-legged, or whatever she prefers).
3. Tell your child to close her eyes.
4. Tell your child to relax her muscles. (You may wish to use part of the yogic sponge exercise in Activity 3N to help your child relax.)
5. Help your child focus on her breathing so that she is aware of every inhalation and exhalation.
6. Tell her to start using her mantra, repeating it mentally every few seconds.

7. Instruct your child to maintain a passive attitude, as described earlier.
8. Keep an eye on the clock while your child is meditating. Continue for a set period of time—two minutes at first, with the goal of eventually reaching ten minutes.
9. Help your child practice the technique twice daily, perhaps in the morning and before bedtime.

Adaptation for Younger Children: Begin gradually by selecting two or three of these steps and practicing them together.

USING SPIRITUAL METHODS

If your child has spiritual beliefs (for example, faith in God or some other beneficent supernatural force), these techniques can be the most effective. We will expand on the spiritual aspects of antianxiety strategies in the next two chapters.

Prayer

For many centuries, prayer has been used to calm overwrought nervous systems. Sometimes people are not even aware of the calming effects that a simple word with a higher power has on their thinking. Since prehistoric times, people have used two approaches to prayer:

1. *Rhythmic prayer.* The person says words intended for a higher power or deity over and over again. The drumming and dance songs of preindustrial societies as well as using strands of beads in prayer by Buddhists and Catholics are examples of this repetitive form of prayer. The use of beads in the recital of prayers has long been known to quiet the nerves and prepare the mind for effective problem solving. In times of distress, the ritualistic repetition of prayers

often brings peace to the mind, mainly through its effect on the sub-cortex of the brain.

2. *Substantive prayer*. In this kind of prayer there is less emphasis on the rhythm of the recitation and more on the meaning of the words. The person expresses thoughts chosen for their ability to bring peace to a troubled mind. This kind of praying causes a refocusing and allows the person to see the bigger picture, to gain a new point of view. This change, which occurs in the cortex, quiets the alarmist messages being sent to the subcortex and replaces them with a sense that all is well.

We think that a fine example of this second type of prayer is one composed in the twelfth century by St. Francis of Assisi.

> Lord, make me a channel of thy peace—
> That where there is hatred, I may bring love.
> That where there is wrong, I may bring a spirit of
>   forgiveness.
> That where there is discord, I may bring harmony.
> That where there is error, I may bring truth.
> That where there is doubt, I may bring faith.
> That where there is despair, I may bring hope.
> That where there are shadows, I may bring light.
> Lord grant that I may seek rather to comfort than to be
>   comforted.
> To understand rather than to be understood.
> To love than to be loved.
> For it is by self-forgetting that one finds.
> It is by forgiving that one is forgiven.
> It is by dying that one awakens to Eternal Life.
> Amen.

The spiritual aspect of the next activity is not necessarily religious, but the repetitive nature of moving and holding the objects on the "worry cord" creates a serene and peaceful mentality that is ultimately relaxing. Even a young child can learn to use a worry cord as a way to quiet her nerves and prepare her mind for effective problem solving. If your child also believes that the objects on the cord are imbued with special properties (for example, if they belonged to a deceased relative), then their efficacy is even greater. There are many possible variations on this activity, depending on your family's spiritual practices and beliefs.

ACTIVITY

Making a Worry Cord

Target Age: 10 to 17
Goal: To find a sense of calm through a spiritual connection
Materials Needed: Five small objects (religious medals, small clamshells, and the like) that can be attached to a cord, and ten inches of smooth, heavy cord

Let your child select the colors and shapes of the five small objects. (Another option is to have your child string the precise number of beads required for religious prayer, as in a standard set of rosary beads.) Sit with your child as she attaches the objects to the cord, and ask her to talk about them as she places them on the string. (Help her secure the objects to the cord if necessary.) You may find that certain colors or shapes hold special meaning for her of which you were unaware.

When your child has completed the worry cord, tell her that she can use it in whatever way feels most comfortable. For example, she can feel the objects between her fingers as she listens to and sings a favorite song. Or she can use her beads in the rituals of her organized religion.

Adaptation for Younger Children: Having the child repeat a familiar song from a popular source, such as *Sesame Street*, *The Lion King*, or Barney, may be more effective.

Because the use of beads in public (such as in the classroom) may draw unwanted attention to your child, you might provide her with an unobtrusive substitute, such as a "magical" flat stone. She can turn the stone in her pocket each time she recites a poem, prayer, or other calming phrase.

Creating a "Bank of Goodwill"

No one lives a tranquil life, at least not all of the time, because stressful events inevitably occur. When tragedy strikes, we cannot hope our children will be calm merely by breathing or visualizing. There are times when they will be distraught.

How can you help your child prepare for the really serious stresses of life? Dr. Hans Selye, whose general adaptation syndrome was described earlier in this chapter, believes that we all need to cultivate resources that can help us when the hard times come. We should begin this process of building what he calls a bank of goodwill early in life. When we regularly perform acts of helping and caring for others, those others will stand by us and give us spiritual sustenance that will help us cope in times of need. When faced with critical situations, we draw on this bank of goodwill, which is the only way we can hope to recover our sense of balance and think our way to productive solutions. The techniques discussed in this chapter are useful—no question about it—but when times are especially difficult, it helps if acquaintances consider you a *mensch* (Yiddish for "a truly kind and helpful person"). Acts of kindness and compassion have a way of rewarding the giver as well as the recipient.

What has banking goodwill got to do with an anxious child's ability to relax? It suggests a lifestyle that will foster tranquility. Dr. Selye explains this well:

> Even primitive animals instinctively hoard things that they may need in the future to ensure their own security. The work of accumulating food or building highly organized living quarters is a basic biological drive. . . . it is as characteristic of ants, bees, squirrels and beavers as of the capitalist who collects money to put away in the bank. The same impulse drives entire human societies to amass a system of roads, telephones, cities and fortifications that strike them as useful means of accumulating the ingredients of security and comfort.
>
> In man, this urge first manifests itself when children start to amass matchboxes, shell or stickers; it continues when adults collect stamps or coins. The natural drive for collecting is certainly not an artificial, indoctrinated tradition. By collecting certain things, you acquire status and security in your community. My suggested guideline to earning love merely attempts to direct the hoarding instinct toward what I consider the most permanent and valuable commodity that man can collect: a huge capital of goodwill which protects him against personal attack from his fellow men.

What better way for your child to recover some peace of mind than by doing that which is most natural to her: helping others so that when the going gets really rough, she will have contributed to her bank of good will. As the Crosby, Stills, and Nash song says, "Teach your children well"—to be thoughtful and productive citizens of their community. Ultimately, being this kind of citizen will lead to the only real safety from anxiety there is.

Chapter Four

COPE Step Two

Originating an Imaginative Plan

For All the Wrong Reasons

When Herbie Rozen's dad came home from the factory that day, his elated mother met him at the screen door, waving a light green envelope in her hand. "It's here," she cried. "It's from the contest—maybe we've won!"

Herbie's parents had mailed in an entry form they had clipped from a magazine contest sponsored by the White Owl Cigar Company. The first prize was an all-expenses-paid trip from Herbie's hometown, St. Louis, to the Bronx to watch the Cardinals play the Yankees in the World Series. In St. Louis, winning this contest was about the best thing that could possibly happen to a kid.

"You open it—I can't," Herbie's mother said. Clumsily, his father tore open the envelope. His eyes skimmed the paper, growing bigger as he read. "My God, it's come true—we *have* won—first prize—it's the Series!"

When Herbie learned that "all-expenses-paid" included a plane flight for the family, he was even more excited. He had never been on a plane, so he was nervous, but excited, too. Over the four weeks before their flight, however, his nervousness overcame his excitement. He couldn't stop thinking about all the bad things that could happen when you're flying. On the morning they were to leave, he couldn't eat, and his father guessed that Herbie was anxious about the plane. When Herbie admitted that he was right, his dad decided that humor could eliminate the problem, and he began making flying jokes so that Herbie would see that there was nothing to worry about. Despite his mother's warnings, his father kept up the banter even on the ride out to Lambert–St. Louis International Airport.

There was nothing funny about Herbie's reaction to being on a plane. Even though his parents had let him have the aisle seat, his frightened feelings overwhelmed him, and he began to sob. The stewardess's words could do nothing to calm him. Unable to bear it any longer, Herbie jumped from his seat, pushed past the stewardess, and tore down the stairs to the tarmac. He raced into the airport, stumbled into the men's room, and crouched in one of the stalls. By the time they found him, the plane had left. No amount of talking to him could persuade him to go, even by other means. Because they knew Herbie had been dying to see the Yankees play in the World Series, they could now see that his anxiety about flying was a serious problem. Severely disappointed, his parents decided to give up the trip.

They tried everything they could think of to help him get over it. They read him reports on how safe flying had become. They took him to talk to a pilot who was a friend of his uncle's. They asked his friends to try to talk him out of his irrational worries. Then they heard about a fear-of-flying course that was being held at the airport, and for sixteen weeks his dad drove him out there for the class sessions.

Nothing worked. If anything, his anxiety about flying got worse. The following summer, Herbie and his family went to Joplin, Missouri, to take part in a family reunion at his grandmother's house. It was easy to see that Herbie was not his usual self. Although he participated in the activities, he seemed distant and preoccupied. Concerned by his behavior, his grandmother began to wonder, "Could this be about something other than flying?" Playing a hunch, she asked Herbie if he remembered taking any trips when he was younger. He immediately began to describe a "vacation" he had had when he was seven.

Because his parents wanted him to experience life in the country, they had sent him to his aunt and uncle's isolated farm fifteen miles south of St. Louis.

His grandmother had forgotten about this trip. When she asked him how it had been, Herbie described it as a disaster. The country kids had made fun of him, he had missed his mother desperately, and after only three days of the planned weeklong vacation, his parents had had to make arrangements for him to come home. Herbie remembered himself as being more than unhappy—he had felt mortified and soon came to believe that the names those other kids had called him were really true. And why had this debacle occurred? Because he had gone away to a strange place. "So that's the problem," his grandmother thought. "It wasn't planes he feared, it was going far from home!"

Herbie's actual problem was no longer a specific phobia; it was beginning to mushroom into agoraphobia, although Herbie's family would not have used those terms. His grandmother's imaginative insight led to a family meeting, at which it was decided that Herbie might be weaned away from his travel anxieties in a series of small steps. After successfully completing each of the steps, his family took him to dinner at Ferdinand's, his favorite restaurant. Eventually, Herbie was able to travel further and further from home without undue distress.

There are three lessons we can learn from Herbie's dilemma:

1. Because most anxieties are based on deep-seated, unconscious thoughts, they often appear to be about one thing but are really about another.
2. A person with imaginative thinking traits is more likely to gain insight into the real causes of an anxiety problem.
3. It takes imagination to design a plan that can confront the real cause of the problem and eliminate it.

In this chapter, we take heed of these three lessons, first by presenting activities that help you and your child think more imaginatively. Research indicates that all of us are capable of thinking far more imaginatively than we usually do. If you will try to develop the thinking traits illustrated in this chapter, you will become a more imaginative problem solver more quickly than you might believe. Furthermore, by sharing with your child the activities that illustrate these thinking traits, he can greatly improve his imagination, too.

The second section presents activities through which you and your child can gain insight into his anxiety problem. Each anxious child's faulty thinking is faulty in different ways. An important target of any antianxiety plan should be acquiring new insights into the real sources of your child's frightened feelings. Your child also needs to open his mind to trying new challenges and to having new confrontations with his fears. By developing more imaginative attitudes and thinking skills, he can become more realistic in his perceptions and more rational in his interpretation of stressful situations. The problem-solving techniques covered in this chapter are useful because they will help your child

- Recognize other points of view

- Address his problem from a new platform

- Dare to be more honest with himself about himself

- Push himself to try new experiences that will help him generate new insights, even if doing so is frightening

In the third section of this chapter, we offer some examples of antianxiety plans, and in the fourth section, we describe a detailed plan that we particularly like. It should be clear, however, that these are only exemplars and are not meant to be the "right way to do it." The reason that someone else's plan designs often won't work very well for your child is that every child's experience of anxiety is unique. Your child needs an individualized plan, customized to his own strengths and weaknesses, preferences and dislikes. General planning principles can be useful, and we provide these, but ultimately only you and your child can understand what his needs are, what motivates him, and what level of stress he can handle.

We have learned that the best plans, the ones that really make a difference, are almost always the ones that are made by those who must carry them out. When you and your child design his own personal plan, he will know where it's coming from and why. He will tend to emphasize the strengths of his plan and be less worried about minor flaws. It is more likely to *feel* right to your child because it is more likely to deal with his unconscious, as well as conscious, needs.

One final point: in this chapter you will be introduced to a number of terms used technically by psychologists. Among these terms are *flexibility, stimulus freedom, functional freedom, remote associations, reinforcement,* and *extinction.* We could use plain English to talk about these concepts related to imaginative problem solving, but then you wouldn't be able to read more about them in other sources or discuss them readily with professionals. We will define these terms as well as we can. We believe that these concepts will help you, together with your child, devise one specific plan that has the best chance of getting to the heart of his problem.

USING IMAGINATIVE
PROBLEM-SOLVING STRATEGIES

You should try out most of the activities in this section before asking your child to do them—you will probably need to alter the instructions and, in some cases, the activity itself. Although they are not actual plans for overcoming anxiety, these activities will prepare you and your child to originate a plan.

Flexibility

In the psychological sense, flexibility means the capacity to see the *whole* of the situation. When we look at all the components in a problem and don't just fixate on one of them, we are more likely to come up with an imaginative solution. When people are under pressure, such as when they are taking a test, most seem to latch on to the first decent idea they get and push it as far as they can. For example, on a test of the causes of the Civil War, many middle school students were found to begin discussing slavery as a cause, and they never moved on to discuss any other possible causes. The Asking Questions Test in the next activity gives you and your child a chance to see how imaginative your thinking is.

ACTIVITY

The Asking Questions Test of Flexibility

Target Age: 10 to 17
Goal: To illustrate the meaning of flexible thinking
Materials Needed: Pencil and paper

The purpose of this activity is to get your imaginative juices flowing. Write down all the questions you can think to ask about Figure 4.1—for example, "What is the clown's name?" Do not ask questions that can be answered just by looking at the drawing. Try to ask questions no one else would think of. Time limit: five minutes. Do not read further until you have completed the exercise.

Before asking your child to try this exercise, score your answers. Doing so involves counting the number of questions you asked that fall into clearly different categories. Analysis of several thousand

Figure 4.1. The Asking Questions Test.

responses to this test determined that there are twenty-one categories of questions, which are listed below. Thus your highest possible score is twenty-one.

For example, questions such as "Where does he come from?" and
"Where did he get those pants?" would each receive one point. However, if you had asked such questions as "What color is his hair?" and
"What does his hair feel like?" you would receive only one point,
because both questions fall into category 8, "hair" (see the list that
follows). The more different your questions are from each other, the
higher your score, and therefore your flexibility rating.

Categories for Scoring the Asking Questions Test

1. Characters outside the picture (for example, the clown's sister)
2. Costume, clothes in general
3. Ethnic factors, race, religion, language, and so on
4. Description of physical characteristics of figure
5. Emotions, thinking, personality of figure
6. Family and home of figure
7. Ground surface (plane)

8. Hair
9. Location, setting of figure and situation
10. Magic
11. Occupation and work figure
12. Pants
13. Physical action related to reflective surface
14. Physical action unrelated to water
15. Reflective surface
16. Shirt
17. Shoes
18. Time, age, past, present, and future
19. Underwater
20. Meaning of picture as whole

A common response to this activity is to ask a question about the clown's hair or shoes and then to ask six or seven questions about that item. This is in accordance with the directions, but it is not as imaginative as someone's asking seven questions about seven different items in the picture. People who do ask wide-ranging questions are said to be flexible and have also been found to be more imaginative than those who don't.

Now ask your child to take this test. When he is done, go over the scoring with him, explaining the principles of flexibility (using your own words, of course). Try to get him to see how this strategy applies to solving anxiety problems. For example, if he is anxious about speaking in class, ask him to describe every aspect of the problem. Point it out to him when he gets overly involved with one aspect of the problem to the exclusion of other relevant factors.

Adaptation for Younger Children: Children as young as five can do this activity. Your child is likely to need to dictate his questions—going through the effort of writing them down could interfere with the flow of his thinking. In addition, you will find it harder to get the importance of flexibility in problem solving across to him. However, this exercise serves to introduce your child to the concept of flexibility in a way that is likely to blossom later.

Stimulus Freedom

The trait known as stimulus freedom is a most useful ability in the fight to reduce anxiety. If you and your child develop this trait, you will both approach his problem with imaginative ideas that would-n't have occurred to you otherwise. Mastering the other strategies described in this chapter will have the same effect. The ultimate goal is for your anxious child to imitate these methods in his own effort to originate an imaginative plan.

Before we explain stimulus freedom, we think it will aid your understanding if you do the next exercise yourself.

ACTIVITY

4B

The Story-Writing Challenge

Target Age: 5 to 17
Goal: To illustrate the imaginative thinking trait known as stimulus freedom
Materials Needed: Pencil, paper, and clock or timer

In writing a story about Figure 4.2, be as descriptive and imaginative as you can. Try to think of a story that no one else would. Give it as imaginative a title as you can. Take up to eight minutes to complete it. You can just create your story in your mind, but if you write it down, you will get more out of it.

After you have completed the exercise yourself and have read the explanation, ask your child to try it; then explain the results to

Figure 4.2. The Story-Writing Test.

him. If taking the test makes him nervous, it will be a good opportunity to help him practice his relaxation techniques.

If your child is too young to write a story, ask him to dictate it to
you and write it down. The only way to judge how imaginative your
stories are would be to compare them to stories written by numerous
other people. Doing so would be impractical, but you can get a good
idea of the quality of the stories written by you and your child by
comparing them to the samples given in the text that follows.

John Dacey and educational psychologist Richard Ripple
employed this exercise in a study of imaginative problem solving
that they conducted with twelve hundred middle school students.
Amazingly, about nine hundred of the students' stories were almost
exactly alike! They went something like this:

How Curiosity Killed the Cat

Once upon a time there was a cat named Tom. He was very curious.
One day he was looking around and spied a suspicious-looking box.
He heard a scratching noise coming from it. He lifted up one side, and

there he saw a mouse named Jerry. Jerry was a fat little mouse, and looked delicious. Without thinking, Tom grabbed Jerry. The box crashed down on him and broke his head [skull, neck, back, or some such]. That was how curiosity killed the cat!

Not very imaginative. The other three hundred stories, however, were decidedly more original, as this untitled example written by an eighth grader shows.

Joe, the chipmunk, was chasing a butterfly. He was starving. The sky overhead was streaked with clouds. The sun when it showed barely filtered through the trees. The burnt floor of the forest made the day seem gloomy. Joe wondered how he was going to get any food. He thought of last night—the men, the monsters. Some had four sharp claws, others had huge round eyes and pointed teeth. Joe was so scared!

Suddenly a bear jumped out of the bushes and was after him. He ran to a stream and started swimming. He was safe—only for a little, but . . . [The story stops here because time ran out.]

What is the major difference between these two kinds of stories? The children who wrote the ordinary stories felt that the lines surrounding the picture restricted them. In effect, they fenced their creativity within a corral of imagined rules.

If you reread the instructions for the exercise, you will see that they include no rules about staying within the lines—in fact, they explicitly encourage vivid imagining. Nevertheless, the majority of the writers in the study assumed a number of implicit limitations, and under those circumstances, it isn't surprising that there wasn't much to write about. The children who wrote the more imaginative stories frequently used the small square in the picture merely as a departure point from which they could travel to other, more exotic lands. Many saw it as a window or a door through which they could exit the picture's frame. Others stretched their imaginations to describe it as a house made of fish, a time capsule, or a player piano. A small number disregarded the square altogether.

Now let's look more closely at the two characteristics of people with stimulus freedom. First, when rules interfere with imaginative ideas, problem solvers who possess stimulus freedom are likely to bend the rules a little to meet their needs. Children who have stimulus freedom would rather err on the side of action. Their play varies; a favorite game or make-believe can have endless incarnations; they reinvent roles and rules. It doesn't matter if "it's not supposed to be like that." The second and more important characteristic of people with stimulus freedom is that they do not *assume the existence* of rules in situations where rules do not exist. Why should anyone assume a rule that doesn't exist? Most people do it because they can't stand not knowing what is expected of them, so to relieve this anxiety they unconsciously make up a rule that eliminates the ambiguity. The puzzle in the next activity often serves to illustrate this tendency. Give it a try yourself before you show it to your child.

ACTIVITY

The Nine-Dot Puzzle

Target Age: 10 to 17
Goal: To understand the assumption of rules
Materials Needed: Pencil and paper

Connect all nine dots in Figure 4.3 with four straight lines, without letting the pen or pencil leave the paper. Don't read further until you have given this puzzle a good try.

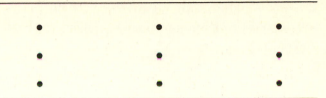

Figure 4.3. The Nine-Dot Puzzle.

Need a clue? Have you or your child been assuming that because the nine dots describe a square, the solution lies *within* that square? In the story-writing task in Activity 3B, most people assume that their story has to lie within the square of the picture. Thus they fail to write an imaginative, interesting story. For the solution to the nine-dot problem, see Appendix B.

Adaptation for Younger Children: Fill a sheet of paper with many dots. Have your child create a drawing with this image. Explain to him that he should be imaginative and draw whatever he wants. See what kind of a picture your child draws. Although most children will associate this exercise with the well-known game of "connect the dots," explain that there are no rules saying that the picture needs to be created that way.

What follows are several mini-activities you can use to help your child become more stimulus free.

ACTIVITY

 4D

Becoming Stimulus Free

Target Age: 5 to 17
Goal: To cultivate stimulus freedom
Materials Needed: None

- Look for even the smallest signs that your child is trying to exercise stimulus freedom. Comment on them
  and praise them.

  "I'm proud of you! You thought up a whole new way
  of doing that!"

  "I agree completely. There's no rule that says you
  have to do it the way everyone else does."

- Help your child recognize breakthroughs by introducing stimulus freedom as a strategy he can count on.

  "Did you notice how the problem disappeared as
  soon as you thought about it in a new way?"

  "Maybe we can free up our thinking about this."

- Play problem-solving games with your child. Take turns
  with him dreaming up imaginary problems and making
  up stimulus-free solutions for them.

  "Good one! You're really letting your mind open
  up now!"

  "This problem you've given me is a real stumper.
  You're going to have to give me some time to get my
  brain around this one!"

Here is an example of stimulus freedom if there ever was one!

The Reluctantly Imaginative Student

A professor was about to give a student a zero for his answer to a
physics question, but the student claimed he should receive a perfect
score and would have if the system were not set up against students.
The question was, "Show how it is possible to determine the height of
a tall building with the aid of a barometer."

The student's answer was, "Take the barometer to the top of the building, attach a long rope to it, lower the barometer to the street, and then bring it up, measuring the length of the rope. The length of the rope is the height of the building."

This is an interesting answer, but should the student get credit for it? On the one hand, the student had answered the question completely and correctly. On the other hand, if full credit were given, the score would reflect a level of knowledge of physics that the student might not possess. It was decided that the student should be given another six minutes to answer the question, with the warning that the answer should show some knowledge of physics. At the end of five minutes, he had not written anything. Asked if he wished to give up, he said no. He had many answers to this problem and was just thinking of the best one. In the next minute, he dashed off his answer, which was as follows: "Take the barometer to the top of the building and lean over the edge of the roof. Drop the barometer, timing its fall with a stopwatch. Then using the formula $S = AT^2$, calculate the height of the building."

At this point, the student was asked what other answers he had to the problem. "Oh," said the student, "there are many ways of getting the height of a tall building with the aid of a barometer. For example, you could take the barometer out on a sunny day and measure the height of the barometer, the length of its shadow, and the length of the shadow of the building, and by the use of simple proportion, determine the height of the building."

"You could take the barometer and begin to walk up the stairs. As you climb the stairs, you mark off the length of the barometer along the wall. You count the number of marks, and this will give you the height of the building in barometer units. A very direct method."

"Of course, if you want a more sophisticated method, you can tie the barometer to the end of a string, swing it as a pendulum, and determine the value of g. The height of the building can, in principle, be calculated. If you don't limit me to physics solutions of this problem, there are many other answers, such as taking the barometer to

the basement and knocking on the superintendent's door. When the
superintendent answers, you say: 'Mr. Superintendent, here I have a
very fine barometer. If you will tell me the height of this building, I will
give you this barometer.'"

The student was not as cooperative as he might have been, but
he certainly demonstrated a talent for imaginative problem solving.

Functional Freedom

Some people have very rigid ideas about how things ought to be. An
example of such rigidity is having inflexible notions about how an
object should be used. A brick, for example, should be used to build
buildings, period. An imaginative person might think of using a brick to
catch worms: you place the brick on the ground, leave it there for two
weeks, and when you pick it up again, there will be worms under it.

Psychologists term the ability to imagine more than one use for
an object *functional freedom*. The capacity to think of lots of imaginative uses for objects can contribute to your child's ability to look
at any situation in a new way. The next activity is another kind of
test you might like to try your hand at. It will introduce you to the
concept of functional freedom.

ACTIVITY

The Two-String Problem

Target Age: 10 to 17
Goal: To master the concept of functional freedom
Materials Needed: Two strings (nine feet long, or shorter if ceiling is

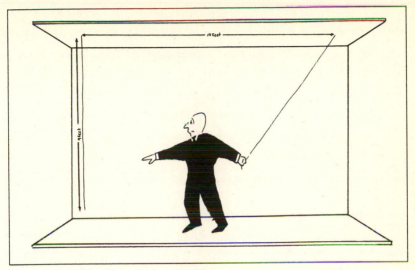

Figure 4.4. The Two-String Problem.

less than ten feet high), adhesive tape, a tape measure, a mouse trap, and a wooden spring-type clothespin.

The best way to set up this exercise is to attach the two strings to the ceiling of a ten-foot-high room, as in Figure 4.4. Each string is almost nine feet long and firmly attached to the ceiling. If the ceiling is lower than ten feet, make the strings shorter accordingly. They are fourteen feet apart. Your goal is to tie the two strings together. Two items are available for use in finding the solution—a mousetrap and a wooden spring-type clothespin—and you may use only one. Neither of them is long enough to be used to reach the second string. No matter how tall you are, you will not be able to reach the two strings, even with either of the two objects.

After you have tried this activity yourself, read the solution in Appendix B and the material that follows here. Then tell your child that standing between the two strings, he must try to figure out how to tie them together, with or without the two objects that are available.

Adaptation for Younger Children: Start by choosing any ordinary object—a spoon, hat, book, or something similar. Take turns with your child so that each of you has thirty seconds to come up with a different use for the object, until you can't think of any more. Start off with easy, ordinary uses, then encourage your child to use his creativity and come up with different, more unique uses. For example, if your object is a book, the first couple of uses might be "to read," "to use it as a paperweight"—by the end of the game, your child might come up with uses such as "balance it on your head" or "cool yourself off by flipping the pages like a fan," and so on.

Many people are unable to solve the problem posed in Activity 4E because they cannot imagine clothespins or mousetraps being used for something other than their usual purposes. Here's an example of what we mean: a graduate student in psychology studied the problem and said, "I've got it! The answer is the mousetrap. You catch a bunch of mice until you get one that isn't seriously hurt. You make a pet of it, then train it to be a 'trapeze' mouse. It will then jump up on one of the strings and swing back and forth until it is able to swing over to you while you are holding the other string!" This solution demonstrates functional fixity: the student believed that a mousetrap could be used only to capture mice. His solution could conceivably work, but it is much more complicated than simply using the trap as a weight.

One young nun in John's class attempted to solve the problem. She decided that the mousetrap and clothespin were really not necessary. Lifting the apron of her religious habit (the long formal dress nuns sometimes wear), she seized the oversized rosary beads hanging from her belt. She swung them over her head while holding one of the strings. The beads caught onto the other string, and, beaming with self-satisfaction, she tied the strings together while those watching applauded! Although this is an imaginative method for solving the problem if you happen to be a nun, it wouldn't work for most of us.

Stimulus freedom and functional freedom differ in that functional freedom applies to attitudes toward *the use of objects*, whereas stimulus freedom applies to attitudes toward *the rules governing situations*. Although the distinction may seem a minor one, each trait plays a distinct role in imaginative problem solving.

ACTIVITY

Get Your Mind Off It

Target Age: 5 to 10
Goal: To use "mindless" activities to practice functional freedom
Materials Needed: None

Remind your child that he can calm his mind by distracting himself with "mindless" activities (see Chapter Three). One of the ways to do this is to count objects in his surroundings. To help him improve his functional freedom as well as give him practice in this calming method, ask him to list objects that could be used as distracters when he is feeling nervous. Here are some alternatives he might not have thought of: the freckles on his arms; buttons on his clothes; repeated patterns on a rug; clouds in the sky; trees he can see.

Adaptation for Older Children: Older children can do this same activity, but they may be even more successful by using peaceful scenic images from their imagination as distracters, such as the ones mentioned in the relaxation activity (Activities 3K and 3L). Not only will they be distracted, but the pleasant images can help calm their anxiety as well.

As your child confronts his fearful feelings as a part of his antianxiety plan, he will need to keep account of each time he succeeds. Watching this number grow will give him powerful motivation to keep trying. Your child will begin to sense his ability to control his own thinking and find that this skill translates into other daily activities as well.

ACTIVITY

Mark That Down!

Target Age: 5 to 10
Goal: To practice functional freedom while learning new ways to evaluate progress
Materials Needed: Whatever object(s) your child chooses for record keeping

Ask your child to think of the most imaginative objects he can that could be used as a way of keeping a count of his successes as he carries out his plan. Here are some objects that he might not have thought of for keeping track of his successes: stones he finds on the ground (dark ones for success, light ones for failures), weeds, or the palm of his hand (which he might mark on with a washable felt tip pen). Older children might use knots on a string, pieces of a puzzle, or the back of a piece of bark (which he might mark on with a nail). Using unique objects to keep track of his successes adds a dose of novelty and sometimes humor to this activity.

Remote Associations

Another important element of imaginative problem solving is the ability to make remote associations. Before we explain what remote associations are, try doing the next exercise. If you think your child could answer some of the questions, have him try answering them, too.

ACTIVITY

Digging Deep for Good Ideas

Target Age: 10 to 17
Goal: To practice functional freedom by learning to make remote associations
Materials Needed: Pencil and a piece of paper numbered from 1 to 15

In the questionnaire that follows you will be given three words and asked to find a fourth word that is related to each of the other three. Write this word on your paper next to the corresponding number. For example, what word do you think is related to each of these three: *cookies, sixteen, heart?*

The answer in this case is *sweet.* Cookies are sweet; *sweet* is part of the expression *sweet sixteen* and is also part of the word *sweetheart.* Here is another example: *poke, go, molasses.*

Slow is the correct answer: *slowpoke, go slow,* and *slow as molasses.* As you can see, the fourth word may be related to the other three for various reasons and in different ways. Now try these.

The Remote Association Test

1.	flap	tire	beanstalk	_____
2.	mountain	up	school	_____
3.	package	cardboard	fist	_____
4.	surprise	line	party	_____
5.	madman	acorn	bolt	_____
6.	telephone	high	electric	_____
7.	hair	income	fish	_____
8.	cream	bulb	heavy	_____
9.	up	knife to	Band-Aid	_____
10.	snow	wash	black	_____
11.	out	home	jail	_____
12.	slugger	belfry	ball	_____
13.	stage	game	actor	_____
14.	Roman	arithmetic	one	_____
15.	cat	color	holes	_____
16.	belle	snow	beach	_____

The correct answers appear in Appendix B.

The originator of the notion of remote associations is researcher Sarnoff Mednick. He believes that imaginative problem solving happens when a person associates ideas already in the mind in unusual, original, and useful combinations. Every image or concept we have in our minds, he says, is associated with other images and concepts. All the thoughts that are associated with a particular idea are arranged in a mental list, so to speak. Those associations at the top of the list are most closely linked to the idea; as we move down the list, the strength of association becomes weaker and weaker. The weaker associations come to mind less quickly.

The list that follows is an imaginary example of an idea and the strength of some possible associations. Ten is the highest rating, indicating that the idea "ride" is closely associated to "bike."

Sample Associations with the Thought "Bike"

Strength	Associated Idea
10	Ride
9	Fun
8	Transportation, red
7	Ten-speed
6	Fast
5	Mongoose
4	The hill on County Road
3	Mary and Jake
2	Wheels
1	Athletic supporter

When people think about solving a problem, they mentally cast about for an association that might serve as a solution. Most of us accept the first idea that seems to solve the problem. Mednick argues that imaginative people are those who go further down the list, searching for more unusual but higher-quality associations to solve their problems. It is these remote associations that produce imaginative products. The poet Marianne Moore put remote associations together in a pleasing new way when she wrote of "the lion's ferocious chrysanthemum head." Although the billowy chrysanthemum is seldom associated with ferocity, the apparent

contradiction is appealing—it makes us see lions in a new and start-
ling way.

Some people have very short lists of ideas that are strongly associated with each other; they can produce only a few associations.
These people are often rigid and dogmatic in their beliefs and tend
to produce little that is imaginative. Others have longer lists of less
tightly associated ideas and are not so threatened by being wrong.
They have the flexibility that encourages the mental search for
remote associations. Some of their freely associated ideas may be
silly, but some produce really imaginative combinations. Most people fall somewhere between these extremes.

Again, if you or your child did not get a high score on the test
of remote associations in Activity 4H, it does not mean that you
are poor problem solvers. Problem solving of course involves many
other factors. However, if you found you *do* have a knack for this
kind of thinking, the odds are that you have a gift that can prove
most useful as you and your child design antianxiety plans.

Lateral Thinking

In his book *Lateral Thinking,* Edward deBono carries the idea of
remote association one step further. He suggests a distinction
between vertical and lateral thinking. Vertical thinking refers to
problem solving that moves in a straight line, a single chain of
thought. Thinking vertically is like trying to reach a solution using
a single short list of mental associations. Vertical thinking is a rigid
strategy that is unlikely to produce imaginative plans.

Lateral thinking involves looking for alternative ways of defining
or interpreting a problem. This approach is more flexible and uses
more than one set of mental associations. As deBono puts it, "Vertical thinking digs the same hole deeper; lateral thinking is concerned with digging a hole in another place." He has contrasted
vertical and lateral thinking in several other ways:

- *Vertical thinking is selective; lateral thinking is generative*. Whereas vertical thinking is aimed at finding the correct solution by following one path, lateral thinking is more concerned with richness than with rightness and thus is more likely to generate numerous pathways of thought.

- *Vertical thinking is analytical; lateral thinking is provocative*. Lateral thinkers seek information not for its own sake but for its ability to provoke or even shock them. The information doesn't even have to be true, so long as it is effective.

- *Lateral thinking welcomes intrusions by "irrelevant" information*. New thinking patterns seldom result from thinking about the problem itself; some information from other sources is usually necessary. DeBono suggests that the more seemingly irrelevant an idea is, the greater is the possibility that it will disrupt the existing thought pattern. This disruption makes the birth of original plans possible.

- *Vertical thinking is sequential; lateral thinking makes mental jumps*. Vertical thinkers proceed through a series of logical steps. That is, each step emerges from the preceding step. Lateral thinkers, in contrast, feel free to make "psychic leaps." They can jump around, using conscious and unconscious material, and do not worry about the logic of their thinking. They know they can come back later to reorganize their ideas and fill in details.

- *Vertical thinking is "high probability"; lateral thinking is "low probability."* Vertical thinking is more likely to give you a fairly good answer, but you need lateral thinking to get a great one.

ACTIVITY

🌀 4I 🌀

Lateral Thinking = Better Thinking

Target Age: 10 to 15
Goal: To have fun thinking in imaginative, unique ways
Materials Needed: None

This exercise is a game that encourages children to think laterally. To set up the game, think of as many common proverbs as possible: "The apple doesn't fall far from the tree," "It takes one to know one," "A bird in the hand is worth two in the bush," and so on. Write down the *first part* of each proverb on a three-by-five card. For example, you would write down "The apple doesn't fall . . .," "It takes one to . . .," and "A bird in the hand is worth . . ."

Put all the cards in a brown paper bag. Each player chooses a card from the bag and has fifteen seconds to come up with an ending. Although most children will be familiar with the standard ending to these adages, the point of the game is to encourage your child to come up with unique, funny endings. For example, if your child picks "The apple doesn't fall," he might come up with the ending "if you're holding onto it really, really tight."

Adaptation for Younger Children: Use nursery rhymes instead of adages. Read the first line of a nursery rhyme to your child, then have him make up the next line, using his own silly rhymes.

Sociodrama and the Use of Imaginative Allies

Sociodrama is a group problem-solving process with a twist. It uses dramatic methods to solve problems. Psychologists have learned that when people try to act out situations that are causing them problems, they often get good ideas about how to solve their problems. It seems that by becoming involved in the playacting, they are distracted from their conscious thoughts about the problem and are able to access unconscious solutions.

ACTIVITY

"The Play's the Thing"

Target Age: 10 to 17
Goal: To invent imaginative antianxiety plans through role playing
Materials Needed: None

This strategy requires a group of people; include members of your family or others whom you wish to involve in helping you originate antianxiety plans. Gather the group and define the nature of the problem. Try to place it in a dramatic setting. Assign roles to the players and improvise a loosely constructed script. Provide props, music, lights, decorations, and so on, all in an effort to create the right atmosphere so that the "actors" will identify with their characters and setting.

As the leader or "director," you have the task of guiding the sociodrama session toward possible solutions of your child's problem, trying not to influence the outcome. As participants act out their roles, you will usually find that a number of excellent ideas are generated.

Your child might think more imaginatively about his problem and his plan for alleviating it if you are able to secure the assistance of a highly imaginative person. Such people can have a unique impact on a troubled mind. It does not matter in what area the person is imaginative. Exposure to the thinking of this person, especially in terms of the problem, is almost sure to prove beneficial.

Sometimes, just by chance alone, we meet someone who has a life-improving impact on us, as the following story describes.

The Itinerant Artist (JD)

Above the garage belonging to the family next door, there was a small apartment. Our neighbors often rented it out to single people for brief periods. Running between our two houses was a long, wide driveway where my brothers and sisters and I played batball. (I am the oldest of nine children, so the lack of players was seldom a problem.) We were out there playing one warm summer day when a thirtyish man came out the door of the apartment. "Hi, guys, my name is Ned. Mind if I play too?" he inquired.

As the oldest, I made the decision: "Sorry, no. You'd hit the ball too far."

"What if I only use my left hand?" he asked, smiling in a way that made us know he wasn't out to show off how strong he was. We let him join the side that had one less player, and with jokes and gentle jibes, he made the game seem much more fun than it usually was.

When I barged out of our back door late the next morning, I found Ned sitting on a small chair in front of the garage, a piece of colored chalk in his hand and an easel standing before him. He was obviously drawing our house, although for a few moments this didn't register, as I couldn't imagine why he would want to capture our plain old place on paper. I got an even greater surprise when I looked at his work. It was our house, all right, but only barely. It was abstract (although I didn't know that then), and it had strange shapes and symbols emanating from it. He explained that he was trying to capture the spirit of our family as represented by the building. He felt it was a powerful energy center, and he wanted somehow to get that down. As I watched, he tried to explain what he was doing. I felt transported by his imagination—I had no idea that complex ideas could be represented figuratively. I had no idea that one individual could have so many unusual ideas!

Over the next five weeks, I followed him around our neighborhood as he sketched the various scenes, scenes that had seemed so mundane to me, scenes that now took on a whole new life as his fingers danced over his paper. And we talked and talked. I told him of my admiration of his skill, and also of my jealousy. By asking questions of me and by commenting on my answers, he gradually convinced me that even though I was only fifteen, I too had a special imagination. I too was full of ideas. He even persuaded me that imaginative thinking isn't all that special. All of us are capable of much more original thinking than we suspect we are.

As his sixth week of living next door ended, Ned gently revealed to me that he was moving on. I was heartbroken. I felt condemned to return to my former life, which seemed so colorless to me now. Simultaneously, I began to get a new vision of things. His words and phrases came back to me, and I got ideas I know I never would have had before I met him. I made up new games to play with my younger siblings. I got involved in several new hobbies. I read voraciously.

He is with me still, these many years later. I wonder what happened to him, and always scan art stalls and museums in hopes of finding his work. I'm sure I would know it. Wherever you are, Ned, thanks!

GAINING INSIGHTS INTO YOUR CHILD'S PROBLEM

As we argued earlier in this chapter, for you and your child to create a plan for reducing his anxieties, you and he will have to gain a better understanding of why he has them. Doing so includes illuminating both his faulty perceptions of the facts and his faulty interpretations of those facts. Why do we say "faulty"? In line with our cognitive perspective, we believe that most childhood anxiety problems result from the child's inaccurate understandings of circumstances and what they mean. Much of the time, the child is not even aware of what he believes to be true. His assumptions must be challenged and redefined. Hence a good plan requires better insights into the actual causes of his anxiety. In this section we provide activities designed to achieve this goal.

ACTIVITY
4K
Eavesdropping

Target Age: 10 to 15
Goal: To gain a more objective view of his strengths and weaknesses
Materials Needed: None

Ask your child to imagine that he is standing in an empty classroom at the end of the day. He is near the door, but he cannot be seen from the hallway. Ask him to imagine that some of his friends are standing out in the hallway and are talking about him. He hears one of them saying, "The best thing about Jim is . . ." Have your child tell you what he thinks this person probably said, and write it down on a piece of paper as the first of a list of positive characteristics. Now another person says, "Well, the thing I like best about Jim is . . ." Your child should tell you what he thinks this person probably said, and you should write that trait down. Continue in this manner until your child cannot think of any more positive descriptions ("he's funny," "he's always willing to help").

Now suggest to your child that there is a different group out in the hallway, and one of them says, "The main problem I have with

Jim is that he is . . ." Ask your child what he thinks this person might have said, and write it down on a list of negative characteristics. Repeat this exercise until he can think of no more traits.

As you can guess, the purpose of this activity is to help your child get a clearer view of himself as he thinks others see him. In reality, the exercise is probably more reflective of what he actually thinks of himself, as he must supply the two lists of traits from his own imagination. You, a relative, or a friend (or a pair or group of you) can discuss these lists with your child in order to help him get a more objective view of what he is really like. This discussion can be especially helpful if you decide to do Activity 4L.

Adaptation for Younger Children: You can adapt this activity by writing a set of adjectives—"funny," "happy," "mean," "friendly," "selfish," and the like—on cards, one per card. Lay them on the floor and ask your child to pick out the "good things that are true about me" and then the "not so good things that are true about me." Complete the activity as above.

ACTIVITY

4L

Why I Am Me

Target Age: 10 to 15
Goal: To understand *why* he gets scared, so that he can come up with ways to alleviate his anxiety
Materials Needed: Pencil and paper

Conduct an interview with your child about the nature of his anxieties. Tell him you're going to ask him a number of questions about why he is scared sometimes and that he should try to open his mind and really explore *all* the possibilities. Here are some sample questions you might ask:

- What are the situations in which you usually feel frightened?

- What are some of the reasons you think you are often scared in those situations?

- Can you think of any other reasons? (Whenever you ask your child for additional information, coax him to give you as many answers as you can without completely frustrating him.)

- What do you think will happen if you stay in a frightening situation for a long time?

- What are some other possible results?

- What do you think would make things better?

- Can you suggest some other possibilities?

- How would you feel about yourself if all your anxious feelings went away?

- Do you think that if we try really hard, we might come up with a plan that could make that happen? Would you like to try?

No matter how well or poorly your child does in this exercise, praise his efforts. Remember that these are probably not questions he enjoys talking about. If you give him praise, he will be more likely to participate the next time you try this activity. (Doing it from time to time usually produces new insights and helps build bonds between the two of you.)

Adaptation for Younger Children: Younger children can do a similar activity using drawings. Ask your child to draw pictures of himself in situations in which he usually feels frightened. Go through each picture one at a time, asking the questions listed for this activity, but in simpler terms. Here are some sample questions you might ask:

- Why do you think you are scared in this picture?

- What do you think might happen to you if you stay in this situation for a long time?

- What would make you feel less afraid?

Now ask your child to draw a picture of himself in situations where he does *not* feel frightened and feels happy and safe. Then you can talk about the following with him:

- Why do you feel happy and safe in this picture?

- Let's try to think about how you can feel this way in times when you are frightened.

ACTIVITY

4M

You Be Me

Target Age: 5 to 10
Goal: To help him see his situation from the standpoint of another person
Materials Needed: None

Tell your child that you want to play a game called "You Be Me." He is to pretend that he is the mother (father, aunt), and you will pretend to be him. He should interview you, asking you the same kinds of questions that you asked him in the activity that preceded this one. Your answers should reflect what you think he is really feeling. After each question, ask him how accurate your answer was.

Adaptation for Older Children: You can achieve the same objective without having to play a role-reversal game. Simply tell your child that you are going to put in your own words how you *think* he is feeling when he is in anxious situations. Ask him if your perceptions are accurate. If they are not, ask him to explain why.

ACTIVITY

4N

The Empty Chair

Target Age: 5 to 10
Goal: To be able to explain his anxious feelings more accurately and to come up with better ways to cope with them
Materials Needed: None

Seat your child and place an empty chair in front of him. Explain that he is to pretend there is a person sitting in the empty chair and that he is the imaginary person. He is to explain to his imaginary self that he understands how his imaginary self feels. He should tell his imaginary self just what it feels like to be in a scary situation. Then he should offer some suggestions to himself about how he should handle himself when he becomes frightened.

Adaptation for Older Children: Have your child talk to himself in a mirror, as if he were another person; his doing so can often help him become aware of his irrational ways of thinking. For example, your child can say to his mirror image, "Why are you feeling this way?" "This anxiety you are experiencing is not based on rational thoughts," and so on.

ACTIVITY

My Memoir

Target Age: 10 to 17
Goal: To understand the roots of his anxiety by remembering the first time he felt anxious
Materials Needed: Pencil and paper

Explain to your child that you would like him to try to understand the roots of his anxiety problem. In this activity, he is to write a memoir of his experiences relating to his fearfulness. Tell him he should drift back in time and try to remember the first time he felt frightened in an anxiety-producing situation. He should write in as much detail as possible about what happened and how he felt about what happened. You'll probably need to ask some probing questions to help him recover as much detail as possible.

Adaptation for Younger Children: Have your child dictate his memoir to you.

To gain a better understanding of how children feel about their family, psychologists often use an instrument known as the Draw-a-Person Test. In this test, they ask the child to draw a picture of his family. From this simple measure, they regularly obtain insights into the child's feelings about the members of his family. For example, the child may draw his mother as being much larger than the other members of the family, indicating that she plays a more important role in his life that his father or his siblings. This next exercise borrows from the Draw-a-Person Test.

ACTIVITY

◎ 4P ◎

Here's What My Family Looks Like

Target Age: 5 to 17
Goal: To foster an understanding of his feelings about his family in order to better understand his anxiety
Materials Needed: Pencil and paper

Ask your child to draw several pictures of the situation that causes him anxiety as he sees it. When he has finished the drawings, look over them with him. Together you are likely to observe elements in the drawings that through discussion will give you insight into your child's anxieties.

CREATING ANTIANXIETY PLANS

We would love to give you a surefire plan that would eradicate your child's problem, but as we have stated, there are no antianxiety plans that always work for everyone. Every child's problem is unique. Furthermore, most children find it easier to carry out plans they have helped design. Nevertheless, we do want to discuss some examples of plans we have known to work well for many children with whom we have worked. Perhaps one of them will serve as a template for your child's plan.

Successively Approximating

The first strategy is called *successively approximating.* This technique can break down most if not all phobias. The term describes a process through which you strive to achieve your goal not immediately but by approximating it in small successive steps. The steps are carefully planned, and if any one step proves too much for your child, you make the steps even smaller. As an example, let's suppose your child has a dread of snakes. Most of us don't often encounter snakes, but some children and adults live in terror of them any time they are in a wood or a field. The following activity offers a set of incremental procedures that we recommend for eliminating this phobia.

ACTIVITY

Winning One Step at a Time

Target Age: 5 to 17
Goal: To use small steps as a way to gradually eliminate anxiety
Materials Needed: A picture of a snake, a two-foot piece of hose or tubing, a toy rubber snake, and a real snake in a glass cage (at a zoo or vivarium)

While carrying out each of these steps, your child should practice his favorite relaxation technique and continue to do so until he reaches a fairly calm state before proceeding to the next increment. The success of this approach depends on his achieving relaxation before continuing, so be sure not to rush your child in any way.

1. Ask your child to think about a snake.
2. Ask him to look at a picture of a snake.
3. Request that he handle a piece of hose while thinking about a snake.
4. Have him handle a rubber snake while thinking about a real one.
5. Take him on a visit to a zoo and have him look at a snake through the glass cage, without and then with a rubber snake in hand.
6. Touch and handle a real snake.

Flooding

In the preceding activity, we suggested going through a series of steps to achieve a reduction in anxious feelings. Sometimes, though, it can be more effective to use *flooding* to confront the anxious situation directly and immediately. By flooding, psychologists mean that the child is placed (or places himself) fully into the situation he most fears.

For example, suppose your child is terrified of getting into an elevator. As suggested by the prior activity, you could help him inch his way into the elevator car; gradually, through a series of steps, he would become able to ride to the top of the building. However, it may be more effective to get the whole arduous experience over at once.

ACTIVITY

 **4R**

Prepare for the Flood

Target Age: 5 to 17
Goal: To lessen anxiety by confronting it directly
Materials Needed: None

According to this plan, you would persuade your child to throw caution to the wind, grit his teeth, and force himself to face his anxiety directly. For example, if he is afraid of riding in elevators, have him ride in an elevator to the top of the building right away. He then rides up and down in the elevator until his tension is reduced to a bearable level. His tension level drops because eventually he burns up most of the adrenaline in his system. As this occurs, he automatically finds himself more and more relaxed. When the amount of adrenaline in his body becomes low, he will no longer be able to be afraid. Most children experience a sense of sleepiness at this point.

You should use great caution in choosing this model plan, however. If your child is not ready for the challenge, this procedure could backfire, and he could become even less willing to confront the situation. If you think he is ready to take the risk, however, it might be the best plan to use.

Floating

Explain to your child that although his anxious feelings may seem to control him, he does have an alternative: *floating*. Psychologist Claire Weeks teaches this to anxious clients with great success.

ACTIVITY

Just Floating Along

Target Age: 10 to 17
Goal: To learn the technique called floating
Materials Needed: None

Tell your child that when he experiences strong fearful feelings, he should imagine himself floating outside of his body, observing himself as though he were ten feet above himself. He should try to watch himself dispassionately as though a separate person. With practice, he can learn to "just float" like this for as long as the anxious period lasts. When he develops faith in his ability to float, he will find that his anxiety no longer has such a powerful hold on him.

Starting from a Safe Place

In his wonderful book *Stranger in a Strange Land*, Robert Heinlein wrote about a magical place called a grokking rock. This was a rock large enough to sit on, located in a secluded spot where a person could go to think. While sitting on a grokking rock, the person would be incapable of thinking self-demeaning or otherwise negative thoughts. Only imaginative, enlightening thoughts could occur there.

ACTIVITY

My Grokking Rock

Target Age: 10 to 17
Goal: To learn to use a "safe place" to relieve anxieties
Materials Needed: None

Tell your child to hunt for a favorite rock or other natural resting place in the neighborhood. (It could be a tree, a bush, or something similar.) Explain that if his imagination is working properly, he can make that rock into a grokking rock. When he is worrying about something he fears is about to happen, if he goes to his rock, he will think of some marvelous solution to the problem. It simply will come to him there. If your child goes there on a regular basis, he could experience a significant reduction in his anxious feelings.

Adaptation for Younger Children: Tell your child to find his "safe place" somewhere inside the house, such as in a tent or fort that he builds in his room.

It's hard to get your courage up when you're frightened about what might happen if you fail. It helps if you have a safe harbor from which to launch. This next activity uses a parent's lap as one such "base of operation."

ACTIVITY

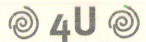

A Welcoming Lap

Target Age: 5 to 10
Goal: To lessen anxiety through the comfort and support of a loved one
Materials Needed: A parent's lap

Ask your child if he feels safe sitting on your lap. Assuming that he does, tell him that one way to deal with a threatening situation is to sit in your lap until he can get his courage up to do something that scares him. For example, it might be telling his grandfather about something that makes him unhappy, such as when his grandfather kiddingly makes fun of him. When he feels ready to take the risk, he can go over and say what he wants to say to Grandpa, and then come straight back to your lap and a hug. The safety of your lap may be just what he needs to perform this brave act.

Adaptation for Older Children: A loving hug can do for your older child what a welcoming lap does for a younger child.

AN EXAMPLE OF A FULL-FLEDGED PLAN: THE FAMILY-DESIGNED RITUAL

We believe that family-designed rituals can make such a powerful contribution that they should be an adjunct to virtually every antianxiety plan. They are also an excellent way to exercise group imaginative problem solving.

People have probably engaged in rituals for as long as there have been human beings on earth; there is archeological evidence of ritualistic behavior among prehistoric families and their communities. By *ritual* we mean a detailed procedure that is faithfully and regularly carried out. Mealtimes, vacations, Saturday morning activities, family reunions, weddings, holidays, birthdays, funerals, first days of school, graduations, family prayers—most families engage in rituals all the time. According to B. H. Friese and C. A. Kline there are eight dimensions common to all rituals. We have adapted their list here:

Dimensions of Every Family Ritual

1. *Occurrence:* How frequently does the ritual occur?
2. *Roles:* How well are the roles and duties of each of the participants defined?
3. *Routine:* Is the activity conducted the same way each time?
4. *Attendance:* Who among the family members is expected to attend? How serious is it to fail to participate?
5. *Affect:* How much are the participants invested in the ritual emotionally?

6. *Symbolic significance:* What meanings do each of the participants attach to the ceremony?

7. *Continuation:* Does each new generation continue the ritual?

8. *Deliberateness:* How much planning and preparation are required to carry out the ritual?

Source: Adapted from B. H. Friese & C. A. Kline, *Journal of Family Psychology,* 1993, 6(3), 290.

Each of these dimensions helps define how well the ritual is developed. Select some ritual your own family holds to, and answer the questions about it on this list. If most of the dimensions are present, you may conclude that the activity is of great importance to your family. That is, if you have gone to a lot of trouble to make sure the ritual is carried out carefully and often, you and your family must care about it a lot. By and large, the more your family attends to these dimensions in designing a ritual specifically aimed at easing your child's anxiety, the better the ritual will serve you.

Studies of family rituals have found clear evidence that families derive significant benefits from these practices. Family rituals

- Help bridge the gap between the generations.

- Provide a sense of identity, especially for teenagers.

- Create a sense of belonging to a larger, caring system.

- Serve as protective guards against risk factors. For example, one study found that children in families that preserve rituals are less likely to become alcoholics.

- Clarify the roles expected of children.

- Help the family navigate change.

- Teach values of living.

- Impart the family's cultural and religious heritage.

- Train participants in practical skills (for example, calming the nervous system).

- Help the family or family members solve problems (for example, by designing a plan for reducing anxious reactions).

- Honor departed family members.

- Create wonderful memories.

From ancient times, most rituals have incorporated what the Greeks came to believe are the four basic elements of life: air, fire, earth, and water. If you have ever attended a Catholic funeral service, for example, you may recall that all four elements are present:

Air: the smell of burning incense that is waved around the casket

Fire: the flames of the candles that surround the casket

Earth: the handful of dried dirt the priest and others toss on the casket before it is lowered into the grave

Water: the holy water used to sprinkle the casket, and the water and wine that are consecrated during the mass

The list that follows gives examples of each of the elements you might use in the ritual you design, as well as the symbolic value of each element.

Element	Symbolism	Examples
Air	Buoyancy	Wind
	Lightness	Balloons
	Freedom	Kites
		Wind instruments
		Speech and laughter
		Bubbles

Element	Symbolism	Examples
Fire	Warmth, destruction	Bonfires
	Passion	Candles
	Magic	Campfires
	Love	Sunlight
	Hypnotism	Spicy food
Water	Baptism	Waterfalls
	Cleansing	Soapsuds
	Change	Oils
	Birth	Rain
	Playfulness	Waves
Earth	Solidity	Soil
	Heartiness	Ashes
	Burial	Rocks
	Darkness	Minerals
	Growth	Plants

ACTIVITY

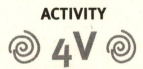

A Ritual Your Child Will Come to Love

Target Age: 5 to 17
Goal: To involve family members in the design of rituals that can increase the effectiveness of antianxiety plans
Materials Needed: Whatever materials your child would like to include in the ritual

For the purpose of illustration, suppose you are in a family in which the father works days and the mother often works nights. You were growing concerned that your family's cohesion was disintegrating, and your young teenager was increasingly anxious about school activities. You hit upon a plan to set aside Friday nights for a ritual dinner and an after-dinner activity.

At first, your teenage child and his six-year-old brother were unenthusiastic, to say the least. Because you encouraged them to help design the ritual, however, they soon became involved and now look forward to participating.

Each week, a different member of your family is responsible for planning the dinner and for outlining the features of the after-dinner activity. The activity usually includes discussion of personal conditions, such as "What was the best thing that happened to you this week?" and "What was the worst? What can we do to help you with that?"

When designing the details of your ritual and when engaging in it, instruct your family to follow three rules:

1. No one may talk unless they are holding the "talking stick" (which can be any object your choose). When the person with the stick is finished speaking, it should be passed to another family member who has raised his or her hand to indicate a desire to speak.
2. No one may criticize anyone else's suggestions.
3. No one should stifle her or his own ideas. Even if you think an idea is silly, every suggestion may serve to stimulate a really good idea.

If you give this plan a try, we believe that your family will feel more close-knit, and your anxious child will be the recipient of a powerful source of help. Don't forget: as always, it is essential that your child be fully involved in the planning.

ACTIVITY

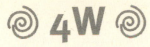

The Magical Medallion

Target Age: 5 to 10
Goal: To use a "magic medallion" to ward off anxious feelings
Materials Needed: 1 c. flour, 1 c. water, 1 c. salt, and an oven

Call your family together (this could include members of your extended family—Grandma or Uncle Harry) and explain that you want them to help your child get over his phobia of thunder and lightning (or whatever your child's phobia). Explain that you're all going to help make a magical medallion from flour, water, and salt.

Mix these ingredients together and form the dough into any shape that your child finds comforting (such as a cross or circle). Bake it at 350 degrees until hard, and when it dries, paint it with any symbols the family and your child deem appropriate.

Next, design a ceremony in which each person participates in imbuing the medallion with the family's good wishes and hopes. All the family members should take turns speaking of their thoughts while holding the medallion in the palms of their hands, for instance. Finally, present your child with the medallion with assurances that if he believes hard enough, the medallion will protect him and make him feel calm during the storm.

Obviously, many variations on the materials, the uses, and the ritual empowering of such a medallion are possible.

Adaptation for Older Children: Your child can use different "good luck charms" that hold special meanings, such as friendship bracelets or other pieces of jewelry, a figure carved out of wood or soap, or a picture of a loved one in a locket.

GUIDELINES FOR IMAGINATIVE PROBLEM SOLVING

As a summary of the ideas we have covered in this chapter, we present a set of guidelines. Numerous guidelines for effective problem solving have been published, and we borrow some ideas from some of these sources. Guidelines can be excellent reminders of how to orient the mind when you or your child intends to produce some imaginative problem solutions.

- Permit your plan to be different from a plan others would think of.

- Tolerate complexity and disorder, at least for a period.

- Use mistakes as positives to help create a supportive atmosphere in which you and your child recognize and accept errors as part of growth.

- Allow time for your ideas to develop. Not all imaginative problem solving occurs immediately or spontaneously.

- Be aware that imaginative problem solving is a multifaceted phenomenon; it enters all intellectual areas, not just arts and crafts.

- Encourage your child's original ideas by being a resource and a provider rather than a controller.

- Create a humorous, supportive atmosphere; it provides freedom and security for exploratory thinking.

- Criticism can be killing; use it carefully and in small doses.

- Ask provocative questions; move away from the search for "correct answers."

- Don't be afraid to start something different!

- Learn to understand the nature of the imaginative mind. We now know that imaginative problem solvers

  Are more sensitive to the existence of problems.

  Have a somewhat greater tendency toward emotional ailments, but also have more self-control to deal with this tendency.

  Are able to be both analytical and intuitive in their thinking.

  Are able to think both convergently (solving problems that have only one correct answer) and divergently (solving problems that have many possible answers).

  Have a higher than average level of intelligence but do not often measure in the "genius" range.

  Are more open to experience and less defensive about accepting new information.

  See themselves as responsible for most of what happens to them.

  Enjoy being playful and childlike; have the ability to toy with the environment.

  Engage more frequently in solitary activities, especially as children.

  Are more likely to question the status quo.

  Are more independent of the judgment of others.

  Are less afraid of their own impulses and hidden emotions.

  Often do not like to work with others and prefer their own judgment of their work to the judgment of others. They therefore seldom ask others for opinions.

  Take a hopeful outlook when presented with complex, difficult tasks.

Have the most ideas when a chance to express individual opinion is presented. These ideas frequently invoke the ridicule of others.

Are most likely to stand their ground in the face of criticism.

Are the most resourceful when unusual circumstances arise.

Are not necessarily the "best" students.

Show an imaginative use of their extensive vocabularies.

Are more original. Their ideas are qualitatively different from everyone else's.

Are like the turtle, in that they only make progress when they stick their necks out!

We realize that this chapter has presented a large number of ideas, many of which are probably new to you and especially to your child. Clearly you're going to have to exercise considerable patience as you and your child learn to master these strategies and activities. We feel certain that both of you will find the reward for doing them well worth the effort!

Chapter Five

COPE Step Three

Persisting in the Face of Obstacles and Failure

@

The Courage of Harriet Tubman

There have been many stories of people who have persisted in the face of agonizing anxiety, but we could hardly find a story about someone more admirable than Harriet Tubman. At thirteen years of age, she was a field slave in rural Maryland. One day, for no apparent reason, an overseer decided to whip the slave standing next to Ms. Tubman, who, although shaking with fear, placed herself between them in an effort to prevent the beating. She had witnessed this atrocity many times and could stand it no longer. Infuriated, the overseer threw a two-pound weight at her and struck her in the head, knocking her unconscious.

Ms. Tubman was bedridden for many months, and being a deeply religious child, she thought long and hard on the wrongs of slavery. In 1849, having learned that she and her brothers and sisters were going to be sold, she decided to try to escape. She has told about the terror she felt as she slipped away and walked by night for hundreds of miles through slave-catching territory. Miraculously, she managed to reach Pennsylvania. Realizing that she had attained safety, she recalled, "I looked at my hands to see if I was the same person, now that I was free."

Working as a domestic in Philadelphia, Ms. Tubman met the leader of the underground railroad, William Still. He had brought many slaves through the secret channels to the freedom of the North. He persuaded her that she could be helpful to him, and although she was terrified of being caught and put back into the horrible conditions that she had left, she agreed to participate. She made at least fifteen tension-filled trips into the deep South and helped an estimated three hundred slaves escape. She even managed to get her parents and six of her ten brothers and sisters out of the abysmal conditions in which they were living. Soon the slaveholders, realizing it was she who was responsible for these offenses against their "property rights," offered the huge sum of $40,000 for her capture. Although she had many close calls, she was never apprehended.

We cannot know whether Harriet Tubman was an anxious person; we can be certain that many times in her life she was terrified, but she never stopped. She never lost a passenger, and she never lost her nerve, and therefore she is a heroine to anyone trying to persevere in the face of anxiety.

Why are some people so unflagging in the pursuit of their goals, whereas others find it so hard to persevere? There are many factors, of course, but when you come right down to it, the difference amounts to one trait: desire.

The treatment of anxiety disorders almost always involves making the problem worse for a while before it gets better. That is the major reason, we believe, that in the midst of carrying out a plan for dealing with their fears, anxious children quite often lose their desire to go on. Their need to protect themselves from frightened feelings overwhelms their zeal for progress, and gradually they lose their drive. We have named this process *drift*. Usually without realizing it, these children begin to drift into self-defeating thoughts. Before they know it, they have lost faith in their plan. But most of them have an asset that they fail to acknowledge: their creative imaginations.

IMAGINATION AND PERSISTENCE

Researchers have noted that successful innovators are exceptionally persistent despite their frustration, even when they are faced with obstacles that might ordinarily be considered overwhelming. Psychologist Mihaly Csikszentmihalyi, in his studies of highly creative individuals, found that they were almost obsessive in their persistence. He describes them as having an *autotelic* personality. The word is derived from two Greek roots: *auto* ("self") and *telos* ("goal"). A person with an autotelic personality is one for whom the goal becomes an integral part of the self. As a result, such individuals have a lot of energy to invest in their work. When they are working, Csikszentmihalyi says they enter a state he calls "flow—a place exactly between boredom and crippling anxiety." This state is variously labeled as being "in the groove," "in the zone," and "in a world of their own." Almost nothing distracts them from pursuing their objective, because they are "on automatic pilot."

Sooner or later, however, all innovative people encounter obstacles to the realization of their dreams. By definition, their ideas typically go against what everyone else is thinking, and therefore they must have great powers of tenacity to continue on the path they believe to be right. For example, the renowned artist Paul Klee did not stop painting in his own way just because gallery owners told him that customers hated his new work and were not buying it. Antonín Dvořák, Michelangelo, Thomas Edison—each is an example of an imaginative person who has doggedly persisted against all odds.

Most anxious kids are above average in creative imagination, too. This is their blessing—and their curse. They have the potential to "hang in there," but their exceptional ability to visualize can also cause them to think up worst-case scenarios. Hence they weaken, falter, and, all too often, give up. When they do give up, they are not just back to where they started. Typically they have lost self-esteem and confidence in their ability to plan and act. The job here in step three of COPE, then, is to encourage the positive side of their creative imaginations while countering the drawbacks. In our view, persistence means developing seven specific strategies:

1. Tolerating ambiguity
2. Learning to handle risks
3. Acquiring a sense of personal courage
4. Valuing delay of gratification
5. Avoiding rigid thinking
6. Avoiding drift
7. Developing a sense of faith

In this chapter, you will gain a better understanding of each of these strategies and learn activities that will both illuminate them and give you ways to help your child practice them.

TOLERATING AMBIGUITY

We have found that most anxious children are creatures of habit. That is how they maintain a careful grip on a world they consider a constant threat. For your child to carry out an imaginative plan to do battle with anxiety requires her to take a step into the deep end of the pool. Attacking anxiety problems means entering the ambiguous zone.

"Of course I want to do the right thing!" said a young teenager with whom we were working. "I'm just not sure what that is. I just can't make up my mind!" It is hard to know what to do in an ambiguous situation. The relevant facts are missing. The rules are unclear. The "right" procedures are unavailable. For a five-year-old, the first day of kindergarten would be an example of an unclear situation; for a forty-three-year-old, it might be a twenty-fifth high school class reunion.

To children, the whole world is ambiguous. Think of an infant responding to a parade of new faces, expressions, sounds, movements. Picture a first grader meeting new authority figures, new expectations for behavior, new ideas. Imagine a young adolescent confronting puberty, academic demands, social pressures. How children react to the unfamiliar depends on how well they tolerate ambiguity. The more poorly they tolerate ambiguity, the more anxious they are likely to feel.

In many ways, raising children can be described as the process by which parents help each child deal with the strange and the unknown. When you embrace life with confidence and enthusiasm, you present a positive model for your child to imitate. If you as a parent were taught to have a low tolerance of ambiguity, you can still encourage your child to reach higher levels, but it takes a good deal of self-awareness to break the cycle (more on this in Chapter Seven).

The best way to measure your child's tolerance of ambiguity is by observing how she reacts to new situations. How does your toddler respond to unfamiliar environments, to unexpected noises or physical sensations? How does your school-age child respond to the procession of first-time events that march through her world—new teachers, open-ended assignments, unscheduled days? How does your teenager respond to the ambiguity of adolescence: "Who am I? Where am I going? What do I value?"

Tolerating Ambiguity Is a Two-Part Problem

Children who have little tolerance of ambiguity usually have two problems. Because they want rules to guide them (in order to avoid making errors), they are likely to slavishly follow whatever rules exist. Worse, they will make up rules when there aren't any, in order to get some kind of guidance. This tendency to assume nonexistent rules is the opposite of stimulus freedom, which we described in Chapter Four. People who have stimulus freedom almost always have a high degree of tolerance of ambiguity.

ACTIVITY

5A

What's Your Problem?

Target Age: 10 to 17
Goal: To deal better with ambiguous situations
Materials Needed: None

Ask your child to think of a problem and then imagine a solution to it. Because your child has an anxious personality, she will most probably ask you to explain what kind of problem you mean. Tell her that the problem should be a real one; for example, it could relate to a situation in school. Possibly the solution could involve one of her teachers. If she still has difficulty completing this assignment, give her more details until she's able to do it. She needs these details because she is probably afraid of making mistakes.

When she has finished describing a situation, examine it to see if she exhibits rigidity about rules or has made assumptions that are unwarranted. Ask her leading questions about the situation that help her say that she is being intolerant. For example, you might ask "What makes you think you would have to do that?" "Do you feel you have other options?" "Do you think the rules in this situation are restricting you too much?"

Adaptation for Younger Children: Begin the exercise with much more specific instructions. For example, say, "Try to think of a problem that happened today while you were playing with your friends during recess. What do you think you might have done to make that situation a little better?" Gradually work toward making the assignment more and more ambiguous.

Familiarity and Stress

Another aspect of ambiguity is the relationship between how familiar a situation is and how stressful we find that situation to be. Imagine a continuum showing the degree of familiarity or strangeness the average person perceives in a situation at a particular moment (see the left column in the table that follows). The face of a brother, for instance, would seem very familiar, a flying saucer very strange. Alongside this continuum extends the degree of emotionality going from equanimity to terror (see the right two columns, one for anxious people and one for imaginative people).

Anxious children often feel that their emotional reactions to strange situations are no different from those of other people. They need to realize that their reactions are often exaggerated. It is also important for them to understand that just because a situation is strange, and therefore ambiguous, doesn't mean they need to consider it threatening.

Table 5.1. The Typical Relationship Between the Familiarity of a Situation and the Emotional Reactions of Anxious and Imaginative Persons.

Degree of Familiarity of Situation	Emotional Reaction of Anxious Person	Emotional Reaction of Imaginative Person
Very familiar (e.g., face of brother)	Equanimity	Equanimity
Somewhat familiar	Interest	Equanimity
Neutral	Excitement	Interest
Somewhat strange	Fear	Excitement
Very strange (e.g., flying saucer)	Terror	Fear

ACTIVITY

"I Guess It's Not So Scary After All"

Target Age: 5 to 10
Goal: To see new situations as exciting, not scary
Materials Needed: Pencil and paper

When your child feels anxious about a new situation that is approaching (for example, her first day of school), sit down and ask her to think about why she is scared. Tell her to give you the number one reason for her anxiety, then numbers two, three, and so on, until she can't think of any more. Write down each reason in order on the left-hand side of a piece of paper. She is likely to say things like, "What if the other kids don't like me?" "What if I don't answer a question right?"

Go through the list, and for each negative, frightening consequence that your child mentions, change it into a positive, exciting one. For example, "What if the other kids don't like me?" can be changed into "What if I make a lot of good friends?" Write these alternative ideas on the right-hand side of the page on each corresponding line. Read the new list to your child and ask her to try to see things in a different light: she can feel enthusiasm with the approach of a new situation instead of fear.

Adaptation for Older Children: Have your child write down her own reasons for feeling anxious. Look at the list and, together with your child, create positive, exciting possibilities out of her negative, frightening ones.

LEARNING TO HANDLE RISKS

An important outcome of tolerance of ambiguity is the ability to take risks. The unknown is a scary thing. People who are different from us may seem dangerous or make us feel uncomfortable. Anxious children often restrict their options just to maintain sameness in their lives; for example, they may be unwilling to travel or may be wary of meeting new people. Fear of risk stands in the way of growth. One of the hardest things for parents to do is to determine what constitutes an appropriate level of risk taking. There are many ways that we can help anxious children become better risk takers. Activity 5C offers a way to help your child understand why a *moderate* level of risk taking makes the most sense.

ACTIVITY

 5C

Lessons from a Ring Toss Game

Target Age: 10 to 17
Goal: To understand why in life, moderate risks are best
Materials Needed: Ten short sticks, a rope to make a ring, a pencil and paper for scoring

Can you remember playing a game called ring toss? In this game, the farther you are from the pin, the more points you score for a successful toss. To carry out this activity, you will need to push ten short sticks into the ground at one-foot intervals. The first pin gets a score of one, the tenth a score of ten. The player gets ten throws. Make a ring of a piece of rope and let your child practice crossing the rope over the sticks. Keep score as she practices.

This game illustrates the continuum of risk taking. After she has made thirty or forty tosses, ask your daughter, "Which pin is the best one to aim at?" She will probably have noticed that you get the most points by aiming at the middle pin. People who aim at the number one position take a very limited risk, but a ringer is worth only one point. Even if they ring the pin ten times, they get a score of only ten. Those who aim at the tenth pin have only one-tenth the likelihood of scoring. Thus even though the tenth pin is worth ten, they're likely to ring it only once, and therefore their maximum possible score is still only ten. If they shoot only at the middle pin, their most likely score would be twenty-five (five successes times five points).

Say to your child, "Although these figures obviously only hold for this particular game, they probably reflect what happens in the real world. That's the way it is in life, too. If you learn to take moderate risks, you're most likely to be successful. Let's talk about what this means when you're trying to deal with scary stuff. What does this ring toss game have to tell you?"

Adaptation for Younger Children: Instead of sticks and a ring, use buckets and a beanbag or a soft, nonrubber ball. (A rubber ball might bounce out of the buckets.) Because young children might not have developed coordination for throwing a ring, throwing a ball or beanbag is easier and serves the same purpose.

Taking Moderate Risks

Children who take either tiny risks or huge risks are less likely to be successful than those who take moderate risks. The child who is socially timid may have just as few friends as the child who is socially reckless. The child who approaches others with a mix of confidence and reasonable caution, however, will be most likely to find rewarding personal relationships.

What determines a child's risk-taking capacity? To a certain degree, genes. Some children seem to clamor for experience. They explore and expand, and when disaster strikes, they may be dazed but rarely daunted. Other kids are more cautious by nature. Hesitant to venture into unfamiliar territory, they want to preview the script before taking the part. This is why it is so important for you to support your child through inevitable periods of failure or rejections.

ACTIVITY

◎ 5D ◎

"I Just Can't Do It!"

Target Age: 5 to 10
Goal: To learn better ways of thinking about taking moderate risks
Materials Needed: None

If your child balks at an activity because she feels she cannot handle it (a school trip, gym class, going to a sleepover), ask her to describe or imagine the experience:

"What do you think it will be like?"

"What was it like last time?"

"What was the worst part about it? What was the best part?"

"How would you make it different this time?"

"Do you think Teddy the Bear would want to go? What do you think Teddy is afraid might happen?"

It may be easier for your child to verbalize "Teddy's fears" than her own. She can tell you that Teddy thinks the teacher likes the other kids better than he likes her. By listening carefully, you can find clues to your child's anxieties. Once you can understand them better, you can use this knowledge to help her be more persistent in her risk taking. For example, anxious children are often blocked because they exaggerate the dangers inherent in a situation. You can help your child become more realistic.

If your child is reluctant to do something, ask her, "What's the worst thing that could happen?" Her answer might be, "They might laugh at me," "It wouldn't work," "I'd lose," or "Everybody'd think I was dumb."

Consequences can become less dire to your child when she can imagine them clearly; she will then be better able to think of alternative responses. Once children begin to realize that they will survive even the "worst thing," they are more willing to take risks.

Adaptation for Older Children: Have your child write down her feelings instead of verbalizing them.

Modeling Moderate Risk Taking

Walk your child mentally and then physically through anxiety-producing events. For example, if your daughter fears riding on a bus, go with her for a ride, letting her watch you deposit the money, choose the seat, and ask the driver for directions. Ask your child questions about what things worry her so that she can describe her frightening expectations and recognize that she can handle each of them, one by one. Ask her "What would you do if (for example, you didn't have the right change)?" "What would you tell 'Teddy' to do if (for example, he missed the stop)?"

One of the best ways to teach moderate risk taking is to model the behaviors that you want your child to achieve.

- Teach by example. Show that it is all right to be wrong. Acknowledge to your child when you are wrong, and demonstrate your healthy attitude. "Oops, Mommy made a mistake."

- Glorify well-intentioned failure. Show your child that failure is her friend and teacher. Failure is a sign of effort, courage, progress, and determination. It is a companion to success.

- Help your child learn to laugh at her mistakes and yours. Most mistakes can be corrected, undone, easily forgotten, or sufficiently apologized for. Why take them so seriously? Instead, show your child how to mitigate the consequences and move beyond them.

In your efforts to cajole your child out of her misery, it's important not to belittle her feelings, though. Acknowledge that failure *can* feel bad. It *is* disappointing to uncover an error, zoom into a dead end, or realize that one must start all over again. However, even young children can be encouraged to look at failure with humor and philosophical acceptance if their parents model these attitudes themselves. Share examples from your own lives: it took eight attempts to quit smoking before you finally stopped; for every sale there are twenty rejections; you invited everyone at the office for dinner at your home and forgot to turn the oven on.

ACQUIRING A SENSE OF COURAGE

Creativity expert Dr. Paul Torrance states that after all the years he has been studying personality traits of renowned innovators, he finds courage to be the most prevalent quality. He further learned that "[h]aving a passionate love for something is probably the key to being courageous."

Being passionate about something can bring great joy, but it also requires an intensity that can cause psychological pain. Our brains are designed to protect us from overload—they rebel against working very hard for extensive periods of time. There are few of us who can endure the psychological pain of this intensity for long, so we prematurely discard ideas that might prove to be of great value if we were to follow them up and work with them. It takes a conscious attempt to summon your courage, especially when you are frightened. The story of the Australian nurse Sister Elizabeth Kenny is an outstanding example of persisting courageously.

Sister Kenny

In 1911, Elizabeth Kenny was working as a "bush nurse," providing the only medical care available to far-flung homesteaders in the Australian outback. She saw a child twisted and in terrible pain; she telegraphed a doctor for advice. The diagnosis she received back was "infantile paralysis. No known treatment. Do the best you can with the symptoms presenting themselves." She came up with the idea of applying wet heat and gently moving the child's legs back into normal positions. Within less than a week, Kenny treated five more afflicted children in the same way, and all of them recovered fully.

A year passed before she was able to discuss with doctors what she had done, and they would not believe her. The accepted treatment for polio at that time was to immobilize patients in casts and splints, sometimes for months, and then fit them with braces or wheelchairs, which they would need for the rest of their lives. Kenny was horrified at the fates of these children and courageously fought for over thirty years to finally have her treatment method accepted by orthodox medicine.

Sister Kenny's courage was tested many times, but her passionate concern for the afflicted children in her care gave her the strength to carry on. This trait has been found to be crucial to the ability to endure trials and carry through to the end. A study of forty innovators who were given the highly regarded MacArthur Award (which grants winners several hundred thousand dollars) found that courage to continue their work in the face of opposition is characteristic of all these winners. They were not quitters, even in the face of insult, defeat, humiliation, despondency, hostility, boredom, or indifference. They continued on, believing passionately in their work and themselves and learning from their failures.

ACTIVITY

Inspiring Stories

Target Age: 5 to 10
Goal: To identify with the failures and unflagging determination of real and imaginary heroes and heroines
Materials Needed: Whatever book(s) you or your child chooses to read

Because they usually possess excellent imaginations, anxious children are often able to identify with stories about imaginary heroes and heroines. Examples of heroes might be Paul Bunyan, Abraham Lincoln, Michael Jordan, George Washington, Superman, Moses, Jesus, Buddha, and Kermit the Frog. Examples of heroines might be Wonder Woman, Althea Gibson, the Blessed Virgin Mary, Wilma C, Joan of Arc, Oprah Winfrey, Amelia Earhart, Pocahontas, and Helen Keller. Any children's librarian could suggest many more.

At your local library, locate biographies and historical fictions that are at an appropriate level for your child. As you read a story, occasionally ask your child one or more of these questions:

"What do you think of the person in the story? Do you admire her? Would you like to be like her?"

"Why do you think she is successful?"

"What could you do to be more like her?"

"How would your life be different if you were more like her?"

Adaptation for Older Children: Ask the children's librarian for suggestions of biographies appropriate for older children. Have your child read the stories herself; she might like to write out the answers to the questions privately.

"Upping the Ante"

Many antianxiety plans we have seen incorporate a reinforcement system. That is, for each increment of improvement (traveling to a new place, speaking in class, and so on), the child receives a reward. When tensions build and your child's sense of courage runs low, such as when she starts to feel "this plan is never gonna work—it's just too hard!" that's when you should increase the reinforcement. In gambling, this is called "upping the ante," meaning raising the stakes of the betting. Sometimes raising the ante is all the child needs to revitalize her motivation and to help her feel brave enough to struggle on toward her goal.

ACTIVITY

Stepping Up the Reward Schedule

Target Age: 5 to 17
Goal: To enhance motivation and thus a sense of bravery through manipulating the reinforcements used

Materials Needed: None

Often it is the case that, as your child carries out her plan, reinforcements she may be getting tend to weaken. With her cooperation, you should experiment with the use of several new kinds and strengths of reinforcement. For example, let's suppose she has a fear of speaking in class. So far in her plan, she has managed to make brief contributions, and when she does, she is allowed to watch the television program that airs at the time she usually goes to bed. Now she has been asked to give a short speech in class, and she is quite anxious about it. Tell her that if she is able to make the speech, you will take her to any appropriate movie that she chooses. Also ask her if there is any other reward she would rather have than the movie. Keep making adjustments until you find a reinforcement that is effective in helping her reach her goal. With many children, simply instituting a new reinforcement, not necessarily a stronger one, revitalizes their motivation.

Tears

Many times we have seen that when a child's courage is running low and the temptation to give up is great, there is a natural tendency to cry. Many children, especially boys, feel prohibited from crying. By failing to access this relief, their emotions are suppressed. Internal conflict results in a diminution of their self-confidence and hence their courage. Only recently, it was discovered that a major component of tears is adrenaline. As you read in Chapter Three, this powerful hormone is responsible for the fight-or-flight response and therefore for numerous physiological reactions to stress. Crying, especially sobbing, removes excessive amounts of adrenaline from the system. Anyone who has ever had a "good cry," whether from sadness or gladness, knows how wonderful it can feel.

It's as though a great weight were lifted from one's shoulders. Depression seems to float away like a cloud, and the future, at least for a while, looks brighter.

Females are usually well aware of this phenomenon, and they tend to cry when they need to, even though it often makes men uncomfortable. Females live six years longer than males, on the average. Females also are eight times less likely to become alcoholic, and have significantly lower incidences of other diseases. Is this because they cry more? Who can say—it does seem likely that crying probably accounts for some considerable portion of the difference.

The societal taboo against male crying is especially powerful among boys in late childhood and early adolescence. At these stages, boys tend to worry about being manly, about not being a "wuss." They hate to be seen crying and feel self-hatred when they do. Why do they feel so strongly about this? Well, ask yourself what comes to mind when you imagine seeing a ten-year-old boy who has fallen down and skinned his knee and is wailing about it. Many people would be embarrassed for him, and if they don't let him know by verbally berating his "sissy" behavior, he will know by the look on their faces. Adults pass on this taboo against crying because of two false assumptions: (1) if someone cries, it means they are cowardly and (2) boys have a greater need to be courageous than girls. We should change this thinking.

Anxious children need to cry. They need to release the pent-up emotions that struggling with their problems always causes. We believe that boys suffer from a double whammy: being anxious is for "chickens," so if you're scared and you're male, you'd better try to hide it. And if it makes you extremely tense to hide it, you'd better not get relief through crying, unless you're in an absolutely private place and no one will see you with red eyes! We need to encourage girls and boys to cry when the stress of carrying out their plan gets too high.

ACTIVITY

◎ 5G ◎

"I Just Need a Good Cry!"

Target Age: 5 to 17
Goal: To encourage a more positive attitude toward crying as an appropriate release of tension
Materials Needed: None

In whatever words you believe will get the message across to your child, explain that tears have a substance in them (adrenaline) that can make us feel very tense. When we cry, we release the excess adrenaline from our bodies, and this helps us feel much more relaxed and better able to deal with our problems. Therefore it is definitely good to cry.

Say to her, "But people who are fearful need to cry more than other people. Other people sometimes make fun of kids who are crying. The other kids just don't understand. We can try to explain to them why we need to cry sometimes, but with some kids, this just won't be enough. Therefore, sometimes it is better if you go someplace where you can have privacy. There you can think about what is making you frightened and let yourself have a good cry. It is a really good thing to do that. When you get through, you'll find that the chemical that was released in your tears no longer makes you uptight, and you can deal with your problem much better."

VALUING DELAY OF GRATIFICATION

The willingness to endure the stress of prolonged effort so as to reap higher pleasures in the long run—that is the essence of self-control. The ability to delay gratification is what makes some people save

money in order to make a major purchase. It is also what makes
some imaginative people spend years on a project without recogni-
tion or reward. As Thomas Edison said, "problem-solving is one part
inspiration and ninety-nine parts perspiration." He demonstrated
his faith in his statement through his invention of the light bulb.
Early in his work, he got the idea of passing electricity through a fil-
ament placed in a vacuum in a glass sphere. Nevertheless, he had
to conduct 2,004 experiments, using different materials for the fil-
ament, before he discovered that carbonized thread would last long
enough to be of practical use.

Many of a child's tantrums, and many of a parent's "No's,"
revolve around the thwarting of immediate gratification: kids want
what they want—now. But in becoming a society that worships
product, we have neglected to teach children the joy of *process*.
Although delaying gratification may sometimes feel like going on a
rough trip, it is ultimately about joy, about the process of working
for, waiting for, and finally rejoicing in a greater pleasure.

ACTIVITY

Be Like a Seed

Target Age: 5 to 10
Goal: To learn an appreciation for the greater rewards that can
come from controlling her desires
Materials Needed: None

In words she can understand, explain to your child the concept of
delay of gratification. For example, you might say to her, "Most of
us like to get what we want as soon as possible. It would be nice if
that could happen all the time. However, it seems like most of the

best things in life can only be had if we are willing to wait for them and work for them. For example, if you would like a little cardboard toy, you could probably buy it with this week's allowance. But if you want to get a really nice toy, you'll have to save up your allowance for several weeks. It's like that when you are trying to overcome your frightened feelings. It took some time for you to learn to be afraid; it could take a while for you to learn not to be afraid any longer. You will have to be patient as you carry out your plan. If you're willing to wait and not give up, you'll surely be successful."

Show your child how plants grow. Plant a seed (a flower or a vegetable—it doesn't matter which) and watch it grow. Suggest to your child that by the time it can be picked, she can have achieved her goal. She can make a deal with herself: "When it blossoms, I blossom!"

Adaptation for Older Children: Explain delay of gratification to her by using experiences to which she can relate—for example, starting to study for a test a week in advance and getting an A versus waiting until the last minute to study and getting a poor grade. She might miss out on a couple of nights of watching a funny TV show, but the long-term satisfaction of the good grade outweighs the short-term satisfaction of watching TV.

AVOIDING RIGID THINKING

A study that examined the open-mindedness of children as they develop compared the performance of first graders with their performance two years later when they were in the third grade. This investigation found clear evidence that although the first graders approached problems imaginatively, by the time these same children were in the third grade, their willingness to entertain new ideas had decreased significantly. Their thinking had become decidedly more rigid. There is reason to believe that this negative trend is even stronger in anxious children.

Another study, which examined a large number of elementary school classrooms, found that approximately 90 percent of the questions asked by the teachers were of the type that have only one right answer. When learning is presented solely in terms of right and wrong, what motivation does a child have to explore ideas and take intellectual chances? When an anxious child becomes rigid in her thinking, she is even more likely to be hobbled as she struggles to free herself from her fears. Thus your anxious child probably tends to worry about what will please authority figures (teachers, guidance counselors, grandparents), rather than feeling confident in her own choices.

ACTIVITY

A Puzzling Solution

Target Age: 5 to 10
Goal: To learn to avoid a tendency toward rigid thinking
Materials Needed: A book or books with puzzles, riddles, brain teasers, or trivia questions

Investigate your local bookstore or library: they carry a variety of books filled with puzzles for children of various ages. This is the kind of puzzle we're talking about: "A tall person is sitting on a stone next to a short person. The short person is the tall person's son, but the tall person is not the short person's father. Can you explain this?" (The tall person is the short person's mother.)

Buy or borrow one of these books and ask your child to attempt to solve some of the puzzles. Make a game of it, and have her stop as soon as she seems to lose interest. You might, for example, ask her to try one or two puzzles before or after dinner each evening.

Adaptation for Older Children: Use brainteasers, trivia games, and conundrums, such as word searches, crossword puzzles, and math or logic games. These encourage imaginative thinking and also help your child develop math, reading, vocabulary, and analytical skills that can make her more confident in school.

ACTIVITY

Where There's a Will, There's a Way

Target Age: 10 to 17
Goal: To develop a sense that when one approach to a problem is not working, there are a number of other techniques that might work
Materials Needed: Book(s) with a hero or heroine

One of the activities earlier in this chapter called for reading heroic stories with your child. For this activity, look for places in the stories where the hero or heroine faces some difficult problem. Read the story with your child and pause at the end of a description of the heroine's dilemma. At that point, ask your child to suggest a solution to the problem. When she comes up with one, ask her if she can think of another. Continue to ask her to generate alternative solutions until she runs out of ideas. Then read on to find out how the heroine solved the problem. After she does this exercise a couple of times, describe an actual anxiety-producing situation that she faces in her own life and ask her to try to produce several new ways to deal with it.

Adaptation for Younger Children: Simply be sure to use appropriate stories that a younger child can easily understand, such as fairy tales and even nursery rhymes.

AVOIDING DRIFT

Obviously, most anxious children want to avoid the painful feelings that their anxiety causes them. Most would give a lot to find relief from these nightmarish experiences. Why, then, are anxious children so resistant to change? One trend we have noticed is that time itself plays a role. At first, your child will try out a new plan with at least some enthusiasm. Eventually the novelty wears off, the bright resolve of the beginning gives way to slippage, and, as we said at the beginning of this chapter, the plan begins to drift. First the child skips little things; in time, she discards more and more aspects of the plan. There seem to be no clear reasons for it; it just happens.

We have found that to overcome the stressful patterns that are emblazoned on the brain of a child like yours, it is necessary to practice over and over again until old habitual patterns are erased. Then the new patterns we recommend are learned well enough that the child comes to have confidence in herself. On the average, it takes at least three weeks of faithful practice for a behavior to become a habit. Just as your child is slowly mastering skills, however, drift is also setting in. You and your child must counteract drift if the plan is to be carried out to fruition.

ACTIVITY

◎ 5K ◎

Slip-Sliding Away in the Movies

Target Age: 10 to 17
Goal: To become more aware of the noxious presence of drift

Materials Needed: Pencil and paper

In most classrooms, it is easy to find students who are drifting. These are the teens who "forget" to do their homework, who fail to study very much for exams, and who are regularly found not paying attention in class. Select one of the many movies about teenagers in school. Don't forget about such classics as "West Side Story," Fast Times at Ridgemont High," The Breakfast Club," "Boys in the 'Hood,'" "To Sir with Love," and "Colors." Suggest to your child that she identify several of the students in the movies she believes are drifting. Ask her to make notes of their school behavior. After she has done so for a significant part of the movies, ask her to describe what she has found. Then ask her to explain as best she can why each of the students is drifting. Finally, ask her if she can see any evidence of drifting in the way that she is carrying out her antianxiety plan.

Adaptation for Younger Children: Have your child watch movies and look for children her age who are drifting. Instead of taking notes, however, she can simply tell you of instances of drifting as she sees them.

DEVELOPING A SENSE OF FAITH

Psychoanalyst Erich Fromm has defined faith as the position we take when

- We know we do not possess adequate information to be sure of what to do.

- We know that it is imperative that we take a position.

Examples of such situations might be getting married, choosing a career, believing in the existence of a supreme being, and taking a stand on why we exist and whether or not there is some kind of existence after death. For the anxious child, an example would be simply believing that her plan will work.

Most of the time when your child feels like giving up on her plan, it is because she has lost faith. We have found that there are three kinds of faith that can influence the successful completion of the plan: faith in oneself; faith in the plan; and faith in the help of a spiritual or higher power. In general, faith in oneself depends on the other two. Children who feel they're making progress in overcoming their anxieties come to have more and more faith in themselves.

As for your child having faith in her plan, we find there's really only one way to get it: as we just noted, she must decide to believe that it will work. Lots of times, in the course of carrying out their plans, anxious children say something like "Sure, I'm doing all right now, but I don't think that I can keep this up. It takes too much out of me. What if I run out of energy? What if I feel like I'm going to faint? What if I lose my nerve?" One parent we know started calling her daughter "What-If Wilma." Some psychologists refer to this kind of thinking as *catastrophizing*: the child starts out by wondering whether something bad might happen; then she begins to believe that it probably will happen; finally she becomes convinced that it is inevitable. As a result of this kind of thinking, she will almost certainly lose faith in herself (thoughts come to her that she can't control), and eventually she will lose faith in her plan and give up.

It would be nice if you could just tell your child to stop worrying about the future, that she can have faith that everything will be OK. Unfortunately, such sentiments are seldom of any help. The best way we know of to forestall catastrophic thinking is through *thought blocking*. This is a procedure in which your child learns that she can control her thinking enough to eliminate self-defeating thoughts. Many anxious children believe that their minds operate independently of their wills. They believe that unwanted thoughts can occur and reoccur to them, whether they want the thoughts or not. To change this belief, they need to practice thought blocking.

When your child gets good at it, she will experience a strengthening of her faith in herself and also in her plan.

ACTIVITY

5L

Hang On 'Til the Timer Bell Rings

Target Age: 10 to 15
Goal: To practice thought blocking
Materials Needed: Kitchen timer or stopwatch

This procedure is best practiced when your child is in the midst of worrying about something. Set the timer for a short period of time (for example, thirty seconds) and ask your child to try to keep from thinking about the troublesome problem. She can try to remember a time when she was really enjoying herself, and tell you why the incident was so pleasant. This usually works well, because it is impossible to feel happy and agitated at the same time. Soon the thirty seconds will pass, and she has had a successful experience. You can repeat the exercise once or twice (then or at a later time), extending the time. It is essential that this exercise be practiced until it is mastered so that it may prove useful in the heat of conflict.

If your child is unsuccessful, use a shorter time, but do not give up. Even five seconds is a beginning. When the first five seconds end, your child can try to get another five. It's like the exhausted marathoner who, near the end of the run, asks herself for just fifty yards, then fifty yards more, until she finally makes it over the finish line. Everyone can block a thought for at least a brief period—then build on that success.

Adaptation for Younger Children: Start with five or ten seconds.

The third type of faith your child may be able to use is belief in the possibility of help from a spiritual force. Spiritual concepts can be a major ally in dealing with anxiety. An old saying goes, "If you believe you can, maybe you can, but if you believe you can't, you can't." If your child can believe that she can get help from a spiritual source, then her chances of dealing successfully with her anxiety are improved.

There are at least six categories of spiritual help that anxious children can access:

1. A supreme being (God, the Great Spirit, the Force, Yaweh, Allah)
2. Spiritual beings (saints, the Blessed Virgin Mary, a guardian angel)
3. Nonreligious entities (the good fairy, leprechauns, imaginary friends)
4. Inspirational places (churches, synagogues and mosques, a "grokking rock," or a secret hiding place, such as a branch in a tree or a hollow in a hillside)
5. Spiritual exercises (saying the rosary, meditation)
6. Family-designed rituals

ACTIVITY

We're Behind You All the Way

Target Age: 5 to 10
Goal: To use family-designed ritual to help strengthen faith in herself, her plan, and a higher power
Materials Needed: Any object(s) your child chooses with which to make her alter and amulet

For the purposes of this exercise, let us assume that your child is afflicted with generalized anxiety disorder—she worries about lots of things. You and your family have decided that designing a ritual in which you all participate weekly could be a big help to her. You have decided further that a "reassurance altar" and an amulet should be the centerpiece of your rite. We suggest you take the following steps:

Start with a family discussion. Ask your child to talk about her fearful feelings and some of the reasons she believes she has them. Ask family members to help design the altar and the amulet, as well as the ritual through which these items will be regularly strengthened.

First design the altar. What shape shall it be? What color? How big? Where shall you put it? (Select a place where it can remain undisturbed for as long as necessary—perhaps several months.) Each member of the family should make suggestions about what items should be placed on it, but your anxious child should have the final say as to which items are actually chosen. Some possible items, chosen for their calming effects, might be the following: a candle, a jar of soap bubbles and a blowing wand, a music box, one of those water-filled globes in which there is a little village and free-floating snow, one of her favorite childhood toys, and a small glass bowl with some incense in it.

Have your child choose or create an amulet (or talisman, totem, good luck charm). One approach would be to take her to a hobby store where they sell a variety of beads with holes in them. Tell her to pick out enough beads to make a twenty-inch necklace. She should make the necklace herself; it then becomes her amulet.

She should wear the necklace all the time (inside or outside her clothing, as she wishes). Each week, during the family ritual, have your child place the necklace on the altar to receive the good wishes of all the family members.

The empowering of the necklace should take place at the end of each ritual session. Before that, the family might hold a discussion with your child about how her week has gone. Ask her what incidents caused her to be frightened and what she did about them. Family members should empathize with her feelings, and if she wishes, they should offer her suggestions about how she might be more successful in dealing with her anxiety in the week to come.

Include in your ritual any practices that you think will help strengthen her resolve to carry on her fight against anxiety.

Adaptation for Older Children: An older child might be more comfortable with a ritual that she does herself in the privacy of her own room. The beaded necklace can still work well as her amulet, but the altar in her ritual might be a small, special box that she keeps on the desk in her room and in which she puts the necklace at night.

In this chapter, we have suggested numerous strategies that you might use to help your child persist in her plan in the face of adversity. Probably the most important strategy, however, is to let her know that you will continue to support her, as nonjudgmentally as you can, for as long as she keeps trying.

Chapter Six

COPE Step Four

Evaluating and Adjusting the Plan

Good Work, Jake!

Jake is a twelve-year-old boy who is frightened by challenges. In most situations where he might make a mistake, such as when he is answering questions in class, he experiences rapid heartbeat and a pounding in his ears, which make it difficult for him to concentrate. This in turn makes him more likely to make a mistake, causing him to feel that "everyone thinks I'm an idiot. It's just better to keep my mouth shut!" Over the years, this problem has been growing worse, and his grades have been suffering. The other students have found him to be "stand-offish." Consequently he has no close friends. As is so often the case with anxiety problems, every time he avoids a tense situation, his life seems to become more disrupted.

Recently, Jake's parents learned about the COPE program from his guidance counselor. With the counselor's help, they have developed a plan for combating Jake's problem, which has a tactic for each of the four COPE strategies:

- *C:* In school, he practices calming his nervous system by visualizing himself stretched out on a raft at the lake his family visits.

- *O:* For four weeks now, at least three times a day, his plan has been to select a time in class when he knew something that he could contribute to the discussion. He has taken his pulse for twenty seconds by pressing his fingers to the side of his neck while using his calming visualization method. When his pulse count has been less than thirty (which if multiplied by three would be a tolerable pulse of ninety), he has raised his hand and made his contribution.

- *P:* So far, his pulse has been more than thirty all but two times he had an idea. He has begun to doubt whether the plan will ever really work, but so far he has kept with it because he receives a movie ticket from his mom at the end of each week if he can honestly say he gave it a try three times each day.

- *E:* Jake uses three types of evaluation every time he chooses to try his plan: (1) He writes down his pulse when he feels that he might be able to participate in class; (2) he rates the pounding in his ears on a scale from one to ten, and also jots that down; (3) he notes whether or not he spoke in class and how it felt.

It has been slow going. Yesterday was a good example. Jake's social studies class was talking about the Revolutionary War battle of Bunker Hill. Another student had claimed that because the Americans had run out of ammunition and had been forced to retreat, the British capture of the hill left them the winners. Jake had made a careful study of the battle, however, and had learned that although the Americans lost three hundred soldiers, the British losses were three times as great. He believed that this difference had strengthened the Americans' self-image as fierce fighters and that it was the most important point in the war. He wanted desperately to share this information—he was sure the other kids would find it interesting—but as he got ready to raise his hand, he became disoriented by the thundering sound of an ocean surf in his head. He tried to relax, but the soothing lake image just wouldn't come. His teacher, noticing the look on his face, asked him if he had anything to add. "No, I guess I don't," he said, staring at his desk. The moment and the opportunity were lost. In short, the plan was not working. Obviously, it was time to reevaluate its methods and to design a better plan.

In talking it over with his guidance counselor, Jake concluded that his relaxation technique was inadequate. He simply was unable to calm himself enough to permit him to make his point in class. Although Jake had chosen the visualization technique himself, he now considered trying something else. His guidance counselor described a more physical method: he would take a deep breath; let it out and hold it; pause before drawing another; tighten his arm and leg muscles, and concentrate on feeling his heart slow down. This approach virtually guarantees a slower pulse.

The very first time he tried it, Jake noticed a definite decrease in the loudness of the pounding in his ears. It seemed like a miracle! At first he did not trust it enough to actually speak in class, but each time he practiced it, he became a little more successful at quieting his nervous system. Two weeks into the plan, he was ready to volunteer. The teacher asked, "Who has the product of 371 times 56?" Multiplication was Jake's forte, and he completed the calculation quickly. Taking the plunge, he raised his hand. As the teacher called on him, his heart rate did accelerate quite a bit, but it did not seriously impede him. "It's 20,766!" he managed to say. The teacher's congratulatory smile and "Good work, Jake" gave him a greater thrill than he had imagined. His anxiety was quickly replaced by a surging sense of joy. This new plan was much more effective, and soon Jake was a regular contributor in his classes.

HOW TO EVALUATE PLANS

Of all the four steps in the COPE program, this is the one that we find anxious children performing least well. It is definitely the step they are most likely to overlook. Nevertheless, it is just as important to their eventual success as the other three.

Why are people so prone to disregard evaluation? Probably the nature of anxiety itself is at fault. Fear is such an unpleasant, noxious feeling. To use the metaphor of a toothache, most of us are willing to take action to relieve the pain of a decaying or broken tooth, but the last thing we want to do is think about it! Ideally, we would like a dentist to come to our house, brush on some magic pain eliminator, and then with a touch of a special sorcerer's tool, make everything all better.

Anxious children typically feel this way about their fearfulness. Dwelling on their feelings, even in an attempt to make their anxiety-fighting plan work better, is about the last thing they want to do. Unfortunately, we don't know of any evaluation techniques that free the child from paying attention to the process. Having someone else observe the child, which is a technique that switches the task of evaluating from the child to another person, can reduce the child's self-consciousness, but self-consciousness cannot be eliminated entirely.

In this chapter, we will be presenting two types of methods. Before using either, though, you will probably need to spend some time discussing the need for evaluation with your child. Explain to him that when people are anxious, they just want the feelings to go away. That's why they often accept any solution that seems even remotely likely to help them. The really good plans are almost always the ones that have been custom fitted to the person's needs. Sometimes custom fitting calls for major adjustments to the plan, and sometimes all that is needed is a bit of tinkering. A little tweak here and there, and the plan runs much more smoothly.

The two types of assessment of plans are *formative* and *summative* evaluation. You use formative measurements while the plan is in operation. These measurements usually are designed to provide feedback on how well formed the plan is as it operates. For example, the evaluations might include checks on anxiety level three times a day, in order to learn whether the time of day is having an impact on how the plan is working. Formative evaluation might involve a parent or buddy watching while the child employs a tension-calming technique before facing a frightening situation. The goal is to make minor improvements to the plan as it is being carried out. If you detect major flaws, of course, you can scrap the plan and devise a whole new approach.

Summative evaluation involves a summary judgment on the overall efficacy of the plan. Therefore, it takes place when you believe the plan is completed. Measurement in this case could involve a comparison of your child's scores on an anxiety questionnaire taken before and after the plan has been implemented. Another example is an interview with your child, encouraging him to list what he believes are the positive and negative elements of his plan.

The next two sections describe examples of formative and summative methods, including instructions for executing them and for using the results to improve a plan's operation. Before we begin these descriptions, however, let's look at one other consideration.

THE ROLE OF GENDER AND ETHNICITY IN EVALUATION PLANS

Many studies have shown that in evaluations of anxiety, females score significantly higher than males. That is, girls appear to be more anxious on average than boys. This is true for six-year-olds as well as elderly women. Some psychologists have questioned this finding. They wonder whether females really are more anxious than males in general, asking these kinds of questions:

- Are girls merely more willing to tell the truth when being evaluated for anxiety?

- Is anxiety different for girls, and should it therefore be measured with a different type of test?

- Are girls more aware of their feelings than boys?

A recent comprehensive study of these questions used a very large group of respondents and high-powered statistical analyses, and appears to have supplied a definitive answer: females really are more anxious.

What about ethnic differences? Children of color, for example, have been found to be considerably more anxious than white children. Is this because, being members of minority groups, many of them suffer discrimination and thus have more to be anxious about? Is it possible that there could be genetic differences? Or could it be that tests that are designed by white psychologists do not work as well for children of color? At this point, we do not know the answers to these questions. One admirable approach to the problem is being investigated. This research is examining the properties of a test called the Terry, which asks children to respond to questions about the behavior of an African American cartoon character named Terry. This instrument, which was designed by black psychologists, may help us resolve some of the questions concerning ethnic background.

FORMATIVE EVALUATION

The good news about formative evaluation, evaluating while the plan is in effect, is that once you and your child learn to do it, the process itself can help reduce your child's anxiety. Evaluating the progress of your child's plan as he is carrying it out offers several advantages:

- It helps your child gain perspective on the problem.

- It takes him away from his worries about future dangers back to a concern with the present (called *centering* by psychologists). Concentration on checking progress often also disrupts anxious thoughts.

- Being self-aware tends to breed a sense of self-control.

- Evaluation leads the child to think of himself as a person who "has anxiety," rather than a person who "is anxious." The child comes to see his anxiety as just a part of him rather than who he is as a person, and thus the anxiety becomes more manageable.

- Formative evaluation encourages "How" questions (How are you feeling right now?) and "What" questions (What is the most troubling aspect of your situation?). These promote the sense of being a self-observer. "Why" questions, in contrast, only produce more worrying.

- At its best, formative evaluation amounts to what has been called "watching myself watch myself." When children master this skill, their anxiety levels are always reduced.

In this section, we present activities that illustrate strategies: charting, using drawings, getting help from buddies or from a therapist, using checklists, journal writing, and photography. We hope that as you learn the techniques we recommend, the beneficial outcomes of evaluation will become obvious to you. We feel certain that your child will experience the benefits.

Charting

There are many ways to use charts to keep track of the effectiveness of your child's plan. The next activity describes one example.

ACTIVITY

6A

Three-Times-a-Day Faces Chart

Target Age: 5 to 17
Goal: To identify patterns of anxiety, as well as provide an easy-to-use method of formative evaluation for his plan
Materials Needed: Pencil and paper

Design a chart for your child like the one shown in Table 6.1. José drew one of three faces on the chart three times a day: one at breakfast, one at lunch, and one at dinner. If José's anxiety level was low, he drew a happy face; if moderate, a neutral face; and if his anxiety was high, he drew a frowning face.

When your child fills out the chart three times a day, you may be surprised at the results. For example, most mornings, your child's anxiety level may be high. You might think your child would realize this without the chart, but anxious people are often unaware of their emotional patterns. They tend to repress most information about their problem because they find it too painful to think about it.

Variations: Some children, especially adolescents, do not like to use happy faces for this exercise; they consider this image to be too childish or out-of-date. Any other images will do—for example, partially closed to wide-open doors. Thinking up a good one can be an important part of this activity, one that calls for using some of the creative thinking techniques we discussed in Chapter Four. Ask your child to draw four or five icons that could be used as markers for his chart; then he can choose the one he likes best.

If your child is a baseball fan, for example, he might use a baseball diamond as his icon. If he rates his performance as just OK, he could draw a diamond with first base blacked out. If he feels he did a really good job, the diamond he draws would have home plate blacked out. Images from other sports can work just as well.

Table 6.1. Three-Times-a-Day Faces Chart.

	Monday	Tuesday	Wednesday	Thursday	Friday	Saturday	Sunday
Breakfast							
Lunch							
Dinner							

As a result of using the charting activity, José found that his anxious feelings usually dissipated by noon, and by dinnertime he generally felt much better. This pattern is quite common in anxious children. We think it results from the generation of adrenaline that occurs as people sleep. It is not that the morning time is necessarily more fraught with frightening circumstances. It's just that our bodies are hyperalert because of the large stock of the hormone (adrenaline) surging through our blood. Thus we feel more anxious because we are oriented to feel that way. As the day goes on, we burn up some of our supply just by living, so that when we reach the dinner hour, we tend to feel calmer.

ACTIVITY

Goal Thermometer

Target Age: 5 to 17
Goal: To create a visible representation of the plan's goal and monitor progress toward reaching that goal
Materials Needed: Pencil and paper

You've probably seen those huge mockups of a thermometer on the town green or some other conspicuous place announcing the progress toward some monetary goal. Perhaps the "mercury" in the thermometer registers at the three-quarter mark. The legend underneath implores, "We've reached 74 percent of our objective, but there are only three more weeks to go! Won't you give today?"

Construct a thermometer like this with your child to keep track of his progress toward his goal. There are many ways to do this. For example, you could use the faces chart illustrated in Activity 6A to make weekly notations on the thermometer. You could add up the

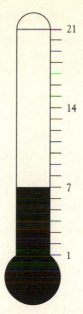

Figure 6.1. The Goal Thermometer.

twenty-one scores for the week, allowing one point for a smiling face, subtracting one point for a frowning face, and no points for a neutral face, and put the total on the thermometer for that week. Ideally most weeks will show some growth toward the ultimate goal. Your child's goal might be a score of between zero and fourteen. (Twenty-one would probably be unreasonably high.) The thermometer, then, would probably look something like Figure 6.1.

At the end of each week, your child fills in the thermometer glass up to the level of his total score for the week, and notes the date next to the level. This way, he records his rate of progress, too. Doing so often helps the child persevere, because progress typically is slow at first and then speeds up. If this is the case for your child, he will note the increased rate and be encouraged by it if he begins to lose faith in his plan.

ACTIVITY

 6C

Pulse Counting

Target Age: 10 to 17
Goal: To evaluate the progress of the plan by recording heart rate at different times throughout the day
Materials Needed: Clock with a second hand

Design a chart to track more objective data, such as your child's heart rate. Measurements such as pulse, blood pressure, and galvanic skin response are also relevant, although the latter two require equipment and technical knowledge, which probably would prove inconvenient for older children and impractical for younger ones.

Your child should be able to count to thirty and read a second hand in order to take his own pulse. As explained in Chapter Three, your child presses the largest two fingers of his hand on his carotid artery at the side of his neck, and as the second hand hits twelve, he begins counting beats. As the second hand passes three, he stops counting and records on his chart the total number of beats he counted in fifteen seconds. He can make these entries at various times of the day or before, during, and after an antianxiety activity (or both).

Adaptation for Younger Children: Take your child's pulse for him and keep a record of it.

Throughout this chapter, we advocate a number of evaluation methods that involve self-evaluation. We should warn you about possible backlash, however. As with any antianxiety method, it is possible to overdo chart making. Sometimes it can backfire, as the next story illustrates.

The Obsessive Pulse-Taker (JD)

I once was asked to help an eight-year-old boy, Cas, who was diligent in his efforts to monitor his antianxiety plan. He unfailingly took his carotid pulse before, during, and after each effort to confront his fear. He meticulously entered these readings on a chart that he had carefully designed.

Unfortunately, instead of getting lower and lower readings, his rates gradually increased. He was very frustrated by this, finally to the point of tears. When his parents came to me, he had been experiencing this problem for about three weeks. When he and I discussed the situation, his plan made sense to me, and, even more important, Cas really liked it. Further discussion uncovered the core of his difficulty. He wanted too desperately to succeed.

Many anxious children are perfectionistic. Whether this causes the anxiety, or the anxiety causes the striving to be perfect, we do not know. At any rate, in Cas's case, he was so worried that his pulse readings would not drop that of course they rose.

When anxiety is mixed with perfectionist leanings, it is probably best to relax the emphasis on evaluation and concentrate on helping your child keep his nervous system calm.

Using Drawings

Psychologists have long understood that a child's drawings can reveal his feelings in ways that words or symbols like numbers cannot. Instruments like the Draw-a-Person Test allow a child to express attitudes and evaluations of which he might not even be consciously aware.

This technique may be adapted for evaluation of antianxiety plans by having your child draw pictures of two kinds: (1) realistic pictures that portray what happened while your child attempted to carry out his plan; and (2) abstract pictures that portray the child's feelings about himself before he started the plan, his feelings during the plan's operation, and even how he feels about the plan itself.

You will have to exercise good judgment in interpreting these drawings. It is easy to overanalyze them. For example, one parent we know was worried because his child would come out from his room having produced drawings that were always colored in black. The father was concerned because he assumed the color indicated a seriously depressed child. When the child was asked why he drew only in black, he replied, "Because that was the only crayon I could find." Nevertheless, you don't need a Ph.D. in psychology to derive a great deal of relevant and valid data from these drawings. Coupled with the child's explanation, they can serve as a most useful evaluative tool.

ACTIVITY

Dream Catchers

Target Age: 5 to 10
Goal: To delve into his true feelings about a plan by evaluating dreams
Materials Needed: Colored pencils and paper

Dreams can often be useful in indicating progress of a plan. Ask your child to try to remember a dream or two each morning as soon as he wakes up. If he lets any time go by before trying to remember his dreams, he is unlikely to recollect what his dreams were about. Have him put a drawing pad and some drawing implements (colored pencils are good) beside his bed, so that he can make one or more pictures of his dreams as soon as he can. Discuss these draw-ings with him and help him figure out what implications they have for evaluating his progress.

Adaptation for Older Children: Older children can write down their dreams or describe their dreams to you, instead of drawing pictures of them.

Working with a Buddy

Anxious children often don't want their classmates to know about their problems. Often, though, your child can make a lot more progress with his plan if he has the help of one or even several of his buddies. When he has come to accept his anxiety problem without a sense of blame and shame, then your child will be able to talk to friends about it in a matter-of-fact way. This allows him both to explain his performance to his friends effectively and also to show them that he expects to be treated like a sane person who has a prob-lem rather than someone who is not acceptable. Also, your child's friends are often in a better position to make judgments about his behavior than anyone else is. Therefore it is often a good idea to try to persuade your child to include a buddy or two in his plan.

ACTIVITY

Daily Interviews with a Buddy

Target Age: 5 to 10
Goal: To use the support of a good friend in obtaining an objective view of progress
Materials Needed: None

Ask your child to choose a friend whom he sees as being completely trustworthy and to explain to this friend exactly what has been happening with him each day. The buddy need not be the same age as your child. The buddy might be another family member or perhaps one of your own friends.

As your child makes this daily report, he will become aware of many details that may well have escaped him in the heat of the day's activities. If the buddy is someone at school or in the neighborhood, your child can make his report in person or over the phone. If the buddy is farther away, your child can use the phone, which may get expensive, or write one letter each day that will be mailed at the end of the week. Older children may find e-mail to be a quick and easy way to communicate with a buddy.

Your child's report should be made in terms of the actions he took and how they worked out, of course, but also should include his feelings. His description of feelings should involve one or the other of two dimensions:

1. Qualitative—a subjective evaluation of his feelings ("I felt scared before I started my plan, and a little sad that I'm the type of person who has to do this sort of thing, but I felt great when things went OK!")
2. Quantitative—how many times or how well he has performed ("I would rate my anxiety level before beginning the plan at about eight. It dropped to around six while I was doing it, and was down to three by the time everything was over.")

As your child speaks to his buddy, he is also hearing himself review how well he has been doing and, through this process, receives invaluable formative evaluation.

Adaptation for Older Children: Older children can especially benefit from the feedback of a good friend, because friendships are so important at this age. The friend should include both the qualitative and quantitative dimensions in his evaluations. Because anxious children expect to fail, they might not think they are making progress; an astute friend can point out qualitative and quantitative progress that the child might not have seen on his own.

ACTIVITY

Long Distance

Target Age: 10 to 17
Goal: To create a special, valued time to discuss evaluation with a close friend or family member
Materials Needed: Telephone, long-distance account

This activity will cost you some money, but it may be well worth it to your child's recovery in the long run. Suggest to him that he make a long-distance phone call to someone he likes but doesn't normally talk to, such as one of his grandparents. The person might also be someone who would not have to be called long distance. Tell him that before making the call, he should take some notes on how well he is progressing with his plan. Then have him call this well-liked person and explain to her what has been happening with his plan. For most children, the fact that this is a special phone call makes him think carefully about his formative evaluation.

Adaptation for Younger Children: Many younger children would feel shy about doing this activity. Perhaps you could have your child call you to give you an ongoing evaluation of his day at school.

ACTIVITY

Muscle Tension Check

Target Age: 5 to 10

Goal: To use massage as a tension reliever that promotes creative thinking and decreases anxiety

Materials Needed: None

Give your child a neck and shoulder rub when he is tense. Turn this massage into a formative evaluation technique by asking him to rehearse going through an anxiety-producing situation while you massage him. Suggest several ideas about how he can better deal with his fearful feelings, and feel with your hands which of these ideas help him be more relaxed as he thinks about the problem.

Adaptation for Older Children: Have one of your child's friends perform this evaluation by giving a shoulder massage and checking for changes in muscle tension.

Working with a Therapist

You may decide that your child's symptoms are not so severe as to require professional help and that you can probably handle the problem effectively with the help of this book. Nevertheless, you may want to engage a psychologist to advise you on the plan you and your child have formulated, to provide encouragement when the going gets rough, and, especially, to offer expert evaluation of your child's progress. Creating an imaginative plan is one step, but there are numerous plans and revisions that will help your child succeed in reducing his anxiety. No one is as well trained to gauge various aspects of your child's progress in reducing his anxiety as a licensed psychologist or social worker. This person need not be a psychotherapist (although they are usually the best-trained individuals in this field). School psychologists can also offer quite useful judgments.

Using Checklists

A major problem with most anxieties is that they tend to build up to a high level of stress without your child being aware of it. Checklists can help him keep track of the symptoms of his anxiety while he carries out his current plan. Checklists also inform him of the frequency of certain symptoms that may be reoccurring.

Psychologists have learned that once a habit has become embedded in the mind, elements of it will pop up spontaneously, even after the habit has been broken. For example, even when a child has overcome acrophobia (fear of heights), later a picture of a view from a high place might set his heart racing.

ACTIVITY

Here We Go Again

Target Age: 10 to 17
Goal: To cope better when symptoms of anxiety recur spontaneously
Materials Needed: Pencil and paper

Have your child make a list of the symptoms that result from his particular anxiety, such as sweating, shortness of breath, or stomachaches. Instruct him to be on the lookout for them as he carries out the current plan. It would be a good idea for him to consult a checklist of the symptoms, perhaps on a daily basis. Assure him that if a symptom that seems to have been eliminated should recur, it does not meaning he is losing ground. It is natural for this to happen spontaneously. He should find, however, that the recurrences happen less and less as time goes on. You may find that your child is made more anxious by checking on his symptoms; if so, you should discontinue this activity.

Adaptation for Younger Children: Have your child list his symptoms for you; write them down. Very young children could draw pictures of their symptoms with you, such as a pounding or racing heart or a red face.

ACTIVITY

Check Those Notes

Target Age: 10 to 17
Goal: To routinely check on the progress of the current plan
Materials Needed: Index cards and a pencil

Help your child compile a list of reminders of things he needs to do to help him persist with his plan, such as giving himself an internal pep talk before an oral report and reporting to his buddy on how he is feeling. Have him write all of these items on a card. Then as he carries out his plan he consults the card and routinely checks off these aids. If things are going awry, he can't help being reminded, and corrective action can be taken in a timely fashion.

Adaptation for Younger Children: Instead of writing words, use pictures of such objects as a thermometer or a heart to remind your child to evaluate.

Rip That Sign to Pieces (LF)

Often when I was a student teacher, we would have trouble getting the children to be quiet during circle time. One day the head teacher wrote the word *NOISE* in large letters on a two-by-three-foot square of butcher paper and hung it on the wall behind him. He told the class that at the end of each session, they would assess whether they had been quiet, and if they all agreed that they had, he would let one of the students rip a piece off the sign. Sometimes the class did better than at others, but the children were very invested in this goal. The class really got into it and looked forward to meeting the challenge of making the whole big sign disappear. By the end of the week, there was nothing left of the butcher paper.

This practice could be used effectively by an anxious child. If he feels anxious at the start of his day (and many children do, as the result of a fresh supply of adrenaline), he could visualize a sign with the word SCARED on it. Each time he confronts his fears during the day, whether he is successful or not in reducing the feeling, he gets to tear off a piece of the sign mentally. As the sign gets smaller, he imagines that his anxiety is fading away, too. The more he can believe in it, the better it will work.

It can serve as a checklist in a way, too. If he finds it hard to tear off pieces, then perhaps the plan should be reevaluated. Thus the size of the sign at dinnertime can serve not only as a reinforcement for progress made but also as a daily barometer of how well the plan is working.

Journal Writing

There are many ways that your child can keep a journal. He needn't be restricted only to making notes in a notebook.

ACTIVITY

The Peaceful Diary

Target Age: 10 to 17
Goal: To more easily and openly describe feelings about the current plan
Materials Needed: Pencil and paper

In Chapter Four, we described your child's going to his "grokking rock," the peaceful place where he can get good ideas for reducing his anxiety level. This is also a good place for doing formative evaluation of his plan. Once your child has established a routine of going to his grokking rock (perhaps on a daily basis), suggest that he bring a journal to write about how well his plan has been working. He should be able to write more freely because he is in a place where he has already trained himself to be calm. Leaning against the rock should encourage him to be reflective and to take a more objective view of himself and how he has been doing.

Adaptation for Younger Children: Ask your child to use his safe place inside the house (fort, tent, secret hideaway) to think about his plans, then to share these thoughts with you.

ACTIVITY

A Very Personal Letter

Target Age: 10 to 17
Goal: To gain a different perspective on the evaluation of the current plan
Materials Needed: Pencil and paper

Suggest to your child that he write himself a letter describing in detail how well his antianxiety plan has been working. He should then mail it to himself. When he opens it a few days later, he may discover that his evaluations were colored by his emotions at the moment. With the passage of time, he may view the situation with a less jaundiced eye. If he gets tired of writing letters to himself, have him write a poem about his experiences or draw a picture or cartoon, and mail that.

Adaptation for Younger Children: Write down your child's thoughts as he says them; read the list back to him a couple of days later.

ACTIVITY

Tape It Now

Target Age: 10 to 17
Goal: To produce a detailed account of feelings about anxiety
Materials Needed: Cassette recorder

An alternative to writing down feelings is speaking into a tape recorder. It might be a good idea to buy your child a microcassette tape recorder so that he can make note of his progress immediately after an episode of challenging his anxious feelings. Your child can save the tapes to listen to his feelings from times past, or he may feel empowered by erasing the tapes, symbolically erasing the anxiety.

Adaptation for Younger Children: Buy a cassette player made for younger children that is easy to use and nonbreakable.

Photography

Cameras can be useful adjuncts to any formative evaluation approach. There are many uses for snapshots. Photography is an especially productive tool when dealing with social phobias. You can tailor the photography to your child's interests and aspirations by positioning yourself unobtrusively at some social situation to get pictures of your child's performance under stress.

ACTIVITY

6M

Candid Camera

Target Age: 5 to 17
Goal: To get a more objective view of how he handles himself when he feels anxious
Materials Needed: Camera

Suppose that your child has performance anxiety—for example, he finds it very difficult to speak in public. As surreptitiously as you can, take pictures of him while he is in the midst of combating this phobia. If you possibly can, do it so that he is unaware of it. Also, if possible, take pictures from behind him so that the picture includes the audience.

Show your child the snapshots you have taken and ask him to analyze the expressions he sees on his face. Ask him to describe his body language and whether or not he sees anything in the reaction of his audience. These judgments should help him get a more objective conception of his performance.

SUMMATIVE EVALUATION

Just as it is important to check regularly on your child's progress, it is also essential that you and he make a careful analysis of the degree to which he has reduced his anxiety when he has finished carrying out his plan. In other words, this evaluation involves an overall summary judgment of how well the plan worked, once it has been completed according to your own time frame. There are many ways to do this evaluation; it is probably wise to use more than one technique so that your child can achieve the depth of understanding he needs to grow from his experience.

Being Objective

Psychologists call anxiety the invisible problem. The symptoms are often not apparent. Your child is even more likely than an adult to have an exaggerated sense of how obvious his internal state is to others. That's why the next exercise can make a big difference in helping him get a more objective view of his actual performance.

ACTIVITY

6N

The Video Camera Doesn't Lie!

Target Age: 5 to 17
Goal: To view reactions to anxious situations more accurately
Materials Needed: Video camera

If you don't own a video camera, you should be able to borrow or rent one. Capturing your child's performance may be difficult because, fearing failure, he may not want to be taped. Overcoming this problem will require some ingenuity on your part. You could film the action from a concealed position. Alternatively, you might be able to conceal the video camera itself by fitting it into a shoebox or briefcase.

Tell your child that you will film the situation more than once and that he will not know when you are actually filming it. Ask him to replay the tape (more than once is better, but he may find it too stressful) and make comments on how he sees himself doing. If you feel he is overly critical, don't correct him. Simply rephrase his criticisms in kinder terms. This will model a more appropriate attitude.

ACTIVITY

6O

The Electronic "Instant Replay" Scoreboard

Target Age: 10 to 17
Goal: To imagine a "successful self" in order to increase confidence
Materials Needed: Pencil and paper

Modern electronic scoreboards usually have a screen on which they can show instant replays of game activity. Suggest to your child that he design an imaginary electronic scoreboard instant replay, featuring him engaging in an action that he finds scary. Have your child visualize himself onscreen, behaving in a relaxed and confident manner, successfully dealing with his anxiety. On a piece of paper, he should describe or draw each scene in the fanciful success sequence. The final scene should be exuberant, with him in some exultant pose. Having this clear "movie" of himself being successful offers him a target against which he can compare his actual conduct. For a teen with computer skills, there are programs that will allow the design of actual mini-movies, which he can use to make this exercise even more effective.

Because anxious children are often also creative, they are good at telling stories. It may be that for your child, telling a story about how his plan worked out, using a fictitious hero for the story, would free him from limitations, such as too much modesty. He might be more objective in this mode than if you were to ask him to write an objective account.

ACTIVITY

 6P

Tell Me a Story

Target Age: 5 to 10
Goal: To become more objective in summative evaluation
Materials Needed: None needed, but a tape recorder would enhance this activity

Ask your child to tell you a story about his plan. You can even tape-record his story and type it up. As he listens to the tape, he can edit it to make it more accurate. When he is done, read the improved version back to him and discuss ways that his plan might have been improved.

Adaptation for Older Children: This exercise might be a little too "uncool" for an older child. Suggest he use video and make a documentary or short movie about himself and his plan, starring himself as the protagonist or a fictional character.

ACTIVITY

 6Q

Hindsight Is Always 20/20

Target Age: 10 to 17
Goal: To recognize aspects of the plan that didn't work well and think of ways to make them better
Materials Needed: None

Ask your child to make a list of suggestions about how his plan could be made to work better if he were to do it again. When he says he is done, encourage him to keep trying until he has exhausted all his ideas. When his list is completed, have him show it to someone (other than you) who has been aware of the plan's operation to see if this person can prompt any useful additions to the list.

Adaptation for Younger Children: Have your child dictate their suggestions to you; write them down.

ACTIVITY

Pretest and Posttest

Target Age: 10 to 17
Goal: To quantitatively assess whether anxiety has decreased as a result of the plan
Materials Needed: Pencil and paper

The Dacey-Fiore Anxiety Questionnaire measures a broad spectrum of symptoms. The best way to use it is to ask your child to fill it out before he commences with the chosen anxiety plan, and then when he has finished it. Score both sets of responses and see whether the posttest yields a significantly lower score on anxiety than the pretest. If so, the results would indicate that the plan was successful.

For items 1, 2, 4, 5, 10, 11, 15, 16, 18, 19, and 20, the scoring is as follows: Strongly agree = 4, Agree = 3, Disagree = 2, Strongly disagree = 1. Item number 9 is called a lie item. If your child agrees with it, he may not be making his responses seriously, or he may be trying to answer only in ways he thinks you would approve. You might want to investigate further whether your child is taking the questionnaire seriously, or whether he is trying to please you with his answers. For the rest of the items (numbers 3, 6, 7, 8, 12, 13, 14, and 17), the scoring is reversed; that is, Strongly agree = 1, and so on. Add up all scores but number 9 to get one overall measurement of your child's anxiety level.

The Dacey-Fiore Anxiety Questionnaire

Read each statement, and think about how much it is true of you. Mark with an ✗ the phrase that indicates how much you think that statement is true about you.

1. I worry a lot.
   Strongly agree ____   Agree ____   Disagree ____Strongly disagree ____

2. I hate to do things where the spotlight will be on me.
   Strongly agree ____   Agree ____   Disagree ____Strongly disagree ____

3. I would say I am not a fearful person.
   Strongly agree ____   Agree ____   Disagree ____Strongly disagree ____

4. A number of things scare me, even though I know they are not really dangerous.
   Strongly agree ____   Agree ____   Disagree ____Strongly disagree ____

5. I am always worrying about what will happen.
   Strongly agree ____   Agree ____   Disagree ____Strongly disagree ____

6. I believe I have a lot of self-control.
   Strongly agree ____   Agree ____   Disagree ____Strongly disagree ____

7. Nothing terrible has ever happened to me.
   Strongly agree ____   Agree ____   Disagree ____Strongly disagree ____

8. I never worry about dirt and germs.
   Strongly agree ____   Agree ____   Disagree ____Strongly disagree ____

9. I have never told a lie.
   Strongly agree ____   Agree ____   Disagree ____Strongly disagree ____

10. Several times a week, I am awakened by scary dreams.
    Strongly agree ____   Agree ____   Disagree ____Strongly disagree ____

11. I enjoy myself more when I am home than when I am traveling.
    Strongly agree ____   Agree ____   Disagree ____Strongly disagree ____

12. I am usually a calm person.
    Strongly agree ____   Agree ____   Disagree ____Strongly disagree ____

13. I am the kind of person who likes to try everything at least once.
    Strongly agree ____   Agree ____   Disagree ____Strongly disagree ____

14. I don't mind being away from my parents.
    Strongly agree ____   Agree ____   Disagree ____Strongly disagree ____

15. I often feel concerned that people are critical of me.
    Strongly agree ____ Agree ____   Disagree ____Strongly disagree ____

16. When I find myself with people I don't know well, I never know what to say.
    Strongly agree ____ Agree ____   Disagree ____Strongly disagree ____

17. I really enjoy going to new places.
    Strongly agree ____ Agree ____   Disagree ____Strongly disagree ____

18. When I leave home, I usually feel like going back to make sure everything is OK.
    Strongly agree ____ Agree ____   Disagree ____Strongly disagree ____

19. I am not too good at doing things, so I don't like to perform with other people watching me.
    Strongly agree ____ Agree ____   Disagree ____Strongly disagree ____

20. Sometimes, for no reason at all, my heart starts pounding and I feel very scared.
    Strongly agree ____ Agree ____   Disagree ____Strongly disagree ____

Once your child has filled out the questionnaire before and after the plan has been put into effect, sit down with your child and compare the two scores. Did he score higher or lower on the questionnaire the second time? If there is not much change, you and your child can think of different plans that will help with his anxiety. This is an excellent starting point for discussion with your child, and it can lead to rich insight into how your child feels about his own abilities to reduce his anxiety.

Adaptation for Younger Children: Read the questions to your child, changing the wording where you believe he will not understand. Mark his answers down for him so you can obtain a total score.

We hope this chapter persuades you of the importance of evalua-tion, and, most important, we hope you are able to use these meth-ods to build a really effective plan with your child. This completes our discussion of the COPE program. In Chapter Seven, we suggest ways that your parenting style can contribute to easing your child's anxiety.

Chapter Seven

How Your Parenting Style Can Help Ease Your Child's Anxiety

@

Parents' Concerns

"Sometimes I feel like wringing Jared's neck and saying, 'Enough already!' We have the same conversations over and over. I could get a tape recorder and just play it back again and again, and it would be the same thing. It gets so frustrating because sometimes I get so sick of it."

"Our trouble began when Henry had a really hard time separating from me when he had to go to school. It got so bad that I had to sit in the classroom with him. I can't do it anymore. I don't think it helps him, my being there. The therapist my son is seeing says that he is a very angry child. But he's not like that at home at all. I mean all boys throw things, don't they? It's normal for boys to play a little rough."

"I finally had what I call my 'validation revelation.' I realized that I had been listening to what Sarah was saying, but I hadn't really *heard* her. Whenever she told me that she was scared I'd always try to downplay things, like, 'It's not so bad,' or 'Don't worry, everything will be OK.' I wasn't acknowledging how really scared she was, nor was I validating what *she* was feeling. I was seeing things through my own eyes and

trying to protect her. I think that if I had stopped and tried to understand how scared she was and how much it hurt her, then I could've
prevented a lot of the pain and worry over the last six months. I feel
like a terrible mom."

It is normal sometimes for parents to feel guilty. The role of parent is unlike any other job or responsibility, and there are no rules,
guarantees, or guidelines. There is also very little training for the
position. If something doesn't go right in their child's life, parents
tend to feel that it's their fault. Today's world is fast paced and
extremely busy, and parents are bound to feel incompetent sometimes. Parents are required to be teachers, doctors, chefs, inventors,
playmates, and role models at any given moment of every single day.
This is a tremendous amount of responsibility placed on individuals who must struggle to provide the necessary time, energy, and
resources so their children can thrive.

The goal of this chapter is to help you do everything you can to
support and nurture your child so that she may grow into a confident, healthy adult. Working with the biopsychosocial model, we
know that parents have some responsibility for their child's anxiety,
but many factors, such as genetic inheritance and neighborhood
events, are pretty much out of their control. Nevertheless, learning
about your role and how your child may or may not react to it is the
first step in teaching you to focus on her in a different way. This
knowledge can help you adapt your current parenting style to prevent anxiety in your child. It will also help you work with her to
overcome anxieties that already exist.

You may not even be aware that you have a certain parenting
style. Style is a hard concept to define, as it varies from person to
person and couple to couple. Simply stated, a parenting style consists of all the behaviors that parents use in the context of their family, such as enforcing discipline and bandaging knees. The parents'

personal philosophies and values form the basis for these parenting behaviors. Various sources contribute to people's parenting style, such as their own parents, their religious beliefs, and the behavior and advice of friends. The decisions that parents make do not occur in a vacuum or "out of nowhere." The experiences they have had over the course of their lives make a significant difference in the way they raise their children.

A number of psychologists have conducted studies that examine parenting styles. In the section that follows we will present the five styles that have been identified over years of research. Later in the chapter, we will discuss how you may unwittingly contribute to your child's anxiety and will explain the steps you might take to shift your own behavior in a way that will help your child. Understanding this information will lead to improved awareness of your child's problems, thus increasing the odds that you will find effective solutions to those problems.

PARENTING STYLES

Diana Baumrind is one of the researchers who have examined the role of parents in child development. Baumrind's research involves observations of parents interacting with their children. She has identified two broad characteristics of these interactions: demandingness and responsiveness. *Demandingness* refers to the standards parents set for their children and their expectations that children will meet those standards. It follows that high expectations are often associated with stiffer consequences if the expectations are not met. Some parents set high standards, others demand little.

Responsiveness refers to acceptance of the child for who she is, as reflected in candid discussions where there is an open give-and-take between parents and their child. Some parents are willing to listen to their child carefully. They consider their child's point of view when making decisions or resolving conflicts. Other parents reject their child's opinions and neglect to consider her as an individual who contributes to the family as a whole. Baumrind has found no parents who are completely responsive or unresponsive. What she has found are multiple combinations of demandingness and responsiveness that result in three distinct parenting styles: authoritarian, permissive, and authoritative. Two other styles, which we will discuss later, are called democratic and nurturing parenting.

Authoritarian Parenting

Parents who use the authoritarian style are highly demanding and highly unresponsive. This style is characterized by a "my way or the highway" mentality; these parents emphasize conformity and obedience and at the same time are unwilling to see the child's point of view. Parents (in a two-parent household) have two votes and their child none. Children are expected to accept their parents' decisions without question, and punishment usually follows disobedience.

Baumrind has found that children of authoritarian parents tend to be more anxious and distant. A child who is not allowed to make many independent decisions does not have the opportunity to experience the consequences of success and failure and so has little practice in making good judgments.

Permissive Parenting

On the opposite end of the spectrum, the permissive parenting style makes very low demands on children. Furthermore, it is extremely accepting, either because parents approve of their child's desires (philosophical) or because they really don't care that much (disengaged). In this type of household, the child gets three hypothetical votes and the parents have none. In the first subcategory, parents choose to be permissive because of their philosophical stance regarding parenting. This "hands-off" philosophy allows children to make virtually all of their own decisions, even when they may not be qualified to do so.

Some parents who use this style of parenting believe that children should be able to watch as much television as they like or to have any bedtime they choose. These parents do not enforce curfews or stress the learning of manners. They have a strong belief that when children are given "freedom," they will almost always make decisions that are good for them. They will get lots of practice in decision making. This philosophy has been espoused by the French philosopher Jean-Jacques Rousseau and by the British educator A. S. Neill in his book *Summerhill*, which was popular in the 1960s.

The other type of permissive parenting results not from a personal philosophy or belief system but rather from the parents simply being disengaged. This type of parenting, at its extreme, may be considered neglect, for the parents exhibit the minimal commitment to their children and their role as parents. These parents usually display little emotional or physical warmth to their child, and may even suffer from depression. Aside from providing the bare minimum in terms of feeding and clothing their child, disengaged parents show little interest in their child's well-being. Often, disengaged parents may be struggling with stresses in their own lives, such as divorce, substance abuse, or lack of income, which makes it difficult for them to find the energy and motivation to focus on the needs of their child.

Unfortunately, disengaged parenting affects a child's development in terms of her forming some of the basic building blocks for successful later development, such as attachment, social and emotional skills (for example, sharing, empathy), and self-esteem. If the child perceives that she is not valued as a part of her family, then she may come to expect that she is not worthy of love and respect from others. Baumrind has observed that children who grow up in permissive households are uncooperative when faced with rules imposed by nonfamily members, such as teachers or clergy. These children also have difficulty controlling their impulses, as they have not learned the concepts of patience and self-control. Although it seems contradictory, children who grow up in permissive households tend to crave rules and guidelines, because such structure provides the security and consistency that their homes lack.

Authoritative Parenting

Authoritative child rearing is somewhere between the authoritarian and permissive styles of parenting. In authoritative households parents place reasonable demands on their children and enforce limits and discipline with rational explanations tempered with love. These parents express love and acceptance openly and encourage the child's participation when family decisions are made. Parents in an authoritative household get two hypothetical votes to the child's one vote, because the parents possess wisdom and experience that the child does not. Parents are responsible for the health and well-being of their child and reserve the right to exercise their majority vote if they feel that their decision is in the best interest of their child. The important element of this parenting style is respect: parents respect the rights of their child, and the child respects the parents' input. Baumrind has observed that children in authoritative homes are happy and self-confident. Both boys and girls displayed independence and cooperative behavior.

Why does authoritative parenting succeed where authoritarian and permissive styles fail? One reason is that the rules authoritative parents enforce are not random and illogical but consistent and reasonable. These parents are not necessarily certain that their decisions are perfect, but they are confident that they provide models of desired behavior and that their children are capable of making intelligent decisions. These parents are aware of their child's capacities and set standards for behavior according to their child's developmental level. As we mentioned earlier, Baumrind's three parenting styles are not the only styles that researchers have identified; the next two sections describe two additional styles.

Democratic Parenting

The original research into democracy in terms of parenting styles was conducted by Alfred Baldwin. Baldwin's findings, like Baumrind's, revealed two general factors in the parent-child relationship: control and democracy. Control is similar to the concept of demandingness we have already discussed; democracy relates to the honest communication between parents and their child. For example, democratic decisions are reached by mutual agreement, whereby the parents receive a total of one hypothetical vote, and the child receives one vote. Parents and child are on equal footing in the decision-making process, and the child's input is actively sought and respected by the parents.

When democratic parents choose to enforce discipline, they provide reasons for doing so. In this aspect, democratic parenting is similar to authoritative parenting. The difference lies in the fact that parents and child are equals in the democratic household. Children who are used to getting their own way find it difficult to obey someone else's demands. Baldwin found that although these children may tend to be more rebellious than children raised in nondemocratic homes, they also tend to be highly curious and creative.

Nurturing Parenting

A fifth parenting style, one that encourages a child's creativity, sense of responsibility, and social skills, has been identified by John Dacey and Alex Packer in their book, *The Nurturing Parent*. Their studies of families whose children had been designated by their school systems as one of their top students in creative abilities revealed many similarities among these teenagers. For instance, virtually all of these youth reported that avoidance of their parents' disapproval is a strong motive for their high level of success. These similarities reflected an underlying philosophy held by the parents that they would nurture their child's development every day in as many ways as possible. Whether this philosophy was a conscious choice or an unconscious instinct, these nurturing parents instilled confidence and persistence in their children, which resulted in their abilities to seek out creative outlets and achieve imaginative outcomes.

In terms of the hypothetical votes parents and child hold in nurturing households, the number is zero. Neither parents nor child have a vote in the decision-making process. Rather, the decisions tend to be reached through a constant give-and-take, evaluative process. For example, parents trust their child's judgment because they trust that they have demonstrated fairness as role models.

As a result of this trust, nurturing parents have fewer rules for their children to follow. This was a significant finding for Dacey and Packer when they interviewed the teenage participants of the study, for they observed that the absence of rules did not mean absence of discipline, as is the case with permissive parenting. Nurturing parents do set limits, but they do so indirectly rather than explicitly. Nurturing parents do protect their children from hurting themselves or others, not by making demands but by communicating values and discussing their child's behavior. This is certainly a unique approach to parenting children, and many parents may not feel comfortable with such an open and unstructured system. Remember that what is most effective in one home may not be effective in another household, with another set of parents; ultimately you are the experts who can determine the most comfortable fit between your parenting style and your child's personality.

CULTURE AND CONTEXT

Aside from the characteristics that parents as individuals bring to the parenting relationship, there are factors in the culture and in the child's own personality that powerfully affect her parents' parenting style. For example, it obviously makes a difference whether the child is raised in a rich or a poor neighborhood. Depending on the family's ethnic and cultural background, what might seem permissive in one home may seem authoritative in another household. Parenting styles thus must always be considered as part of the larger context that includes parents' ethnic and cultural background, marital status, financial situation, religion, age, and so on. The interplay of democracy and control nevertheless plays an important role in the child's social and emotional development.

Furthermore, a calm, quiet baby affects her parents differently than does a tense, colicky baby. The match between a child's behavior or temperament and her parents' style is known in psychological circles as *goodness-of-fit*. This term refers to the notion that children are born with certain dispositions, abilities, strengths, and weaknesses that parents need to accept in order to create a home environment that fosters their child's healthy, happy development. But as we have discussed, parenting is not merely a reaction to the child's temperament. The larger cultural and societal values are also important influences. For the parent of an anxious child, it is often difficult to find the right balance between what he wants and needs and what society seems to decree. This can be extremely frustrating, as the following story illustrates.

I Scream, You Scream . . .

We had just had a pretty good family day together at the beach. Our son Kevin had been afraid of the water at first, so he mostly made sand castles with one of the children on the beach. Eventually he went in the water with me, while my wife stood watch on the sand. I could tell she was worried that he would start crying or make a scene, but she tried to put on a happy face and waved to us. I think we may have even caught the moment on video . . . which would be amazing.

Anyway, when we left the beach we decided to stop by the ice cream truck to have a treat, since it was hot out, and who can turn down ice cream, right? Wouldn't you know it, but Kevin's "bomb pop" [red, white, and blue popsicle] dripped on his new white sneakers, and he had a fit! I mean he just lost it! Out of the blue, and his mother and I hadn't even said a word—we didn't even see the drip. So he starts wailing and pointing and saying, "Oh no! My new shoes! My shoes!" We had to pick him up and carry him to the car because he was so upset, and nothing my wife or I said would stop his crying. We told him everything from, "Don't worry, it'll come out," to "We'll get you new shoes," and finally I had to threaten him with punishment to try to get him to stop. I told him that he'd have to go to his room if he didn't stop his crying, but that only seemed to make him more upset.

Finally we just decided to try and ignore him, but the sounds of his sniffling and catching his breath really got frustrating. You would think he was being tortured or something! I know that we shouldn't punish him when he gets out of control like that, but it's the only thing I can think of to get him to stop. He's so sensitive sometimes . . . and it's like, you never know when something's going to set it off. Wham! Out of the blue. How can I help him be less sensitive?

As a parent, you may struggle a bit to find that certain fit between your child's personality and your parenting style. You may be extremely outgoing and adventurous, whereas your child is shy and reserved. You may be afraid of spiders, and your child is afraid of . . . everything else. Differences between you may have more to do with her inherent temperament than anything else. We would simply remind you that children cannot be molded to fit your expectations. You, the parents, are the ones who need to adapt your parenting style to meet the needs of your unique child. Focusing on her strengths when she is facing her challenges is an important place to start. Each child has individual characteristics that mix with those of her parents and contribute to a unique, bidirectional relationship. You may be unaware that just as you affect the way your child responds to you and the world around her, your child affects the way you respond to her.

PASSING ON YOUR FEARS

No parents wish for their child to be anxious. Unfortunately, the best intentions and a loving environment cannot always prevent a child from developing an anxious temperament. As mentioned in Chapter One, some children seem to have a temperamental predisposition toward worrying about things, whereas other children are influenced by their own parents' fears, which they come to internalize as their own.

Parents who have known the challenge of growing up anxious frequently try to prevent such anxiety in their child by pushing her into situations with which she may not be comfortable because of her personality. For example, a mother who struggled with extreme shyness as a child may push her child to participate in activities she missed, such as running for school government or performing. Rather than remember how painful and difficult shyness was for her at her child's age, the mother attempts to mold her child into a confident, aggressive person, which may or may not be appropriate for her child.

Anxious parents often take the opposite stance, and rather than force their child to face challenging situations, they overprotect their child by avoiding situations that they, the parents, consider anxiety provoking. By taking this overprotective stance, anxious parents send the message to their child that "this is something scary," that "this is something to worry about." The child with overprotective parents does not learn to experience new challenges at her own pace and learn from her own mistakes.

One of the greatest pitfalls into which anxious parents stumble is to share their own anxieties with their child in an attempt to empathize with her. There is always the temptation to talk with your child in detail about what you know, but children will come to believe that whatever you say is inevitable. For example, as adults, we know that germs can make us sick, so it is important to wash our hands after using the bathroom or touching something dirty. However, children may become excessively anxious about cleanliness and germs if they are given a detailed account of how Aunt Florence caught hepatitis from a toilet seat and had to receive shots and antibiotics.

Whether parents force their child to face challenges or protect their child from all new challenges, the result is that the child learns to be afraid and insecure in her own ability to cope with her anxieties. Parents need to ask themselves whether they are trying to help their anxious child or compensate for anxieties of their own. The best advice for anxious parents is to learn to recognize their child's own strengths and weaknesses, as well as their own strengths and weaknesses, regardless of their own personal experiences with anxiety.

UNDERSTANDING THE NATURE
OF YOUR CHILD'S PROBLEMS

If you stop and think about the ways parents, teachers, and others unknowingly teach children about fear from the time they are infants, it is surprising that all children are not anxious. The first lullaby parents sing to their babies is usually "Rock-a-Bye Baby," which features the following lyrics:

> Rock-a-bye baby on the treetop
> When the wind blows, the cradle will rock.
> When the bough breaks, the cradle will fall,
> And down will come baby, cradle and all.

Such words are not particularly comforting, but the age of the infant and the manner in which parents lovingly sing the lullaby tend to eclipse the meaning of the words. The words could, however, be affecting the child unconsciously, so especially with anxious children, we should avoid stories and songs that have violent themes.

Older children read fairy tales with violent conclusions and watch television programs that feature kidnaping, fighting, and killing. Every year, children look forward to trick-or-treating on Halloween, a night that celebrates witches, goblins, and all things scary. As children mature, their anxiety shifts from the impersonal to more personal concerns, such as social situations and performing up to others' standards. In Chapter One we presented a vignette from John's childhood, in which his mother used the threat of the river rats to keep him and his siblings from crossing the dangerous train tracks. Be cautious using threats to get your child to behave, as you may be fueling an already anxious mind. Remember that anxious children possess very creative imaginations, which means that they can dream up scary situations at the slightest provocation. When using threats or ultimatums, be sure to consider whether the threat you are making is an imaginary threat or one you intend to keep.

"Good Night" = Sleep Fright

Bridget saw the hallway light through the crack in her doorway, and her eyes strained to catch sight of her mom's shadow. If she saw her mom's shadow in the stream of light, then she knew Mom was still awake and would protect her if the monster came back. But what if the monster came too fast? What if it took her away in the darkness and she never saw her family again?

"MOMMYYYYYYYYYYY!" she screeched.

"Not again," sighed Claire as she put down the remote control. This was the third time she'd spoken to Bridget about going to sleep. Claire hoisted herself off the couch and padded up the stairs to Bridget's room.

"Bridget, this is the last time I'm going to tell you to go to bed," Claire said, agitation evident in her voice. "You've already gone to the bathroom, and it's late. You have to get up for school tomorrow, and you need your sleep. I'm not going to tell you again." Enough with the bargaining routine.

"I'm thirsty," Bridget whined, thinking, "this will keep Mommy near me for a few more minutes."

"Enough is enough, now go to bed. If you don't go to sleep, the monster's going to come out. He likes tired children because they're easier to catch. If you go to sleep now, the monster won't come out," Claire said.

"That ought to do it," Claire thought. "If I can't get her to sleep because I ask her to, maybe this will work."

What Claire didn't understand is that frightening Bridget didn't help the situation. If anything, it added fuel to her already active imagination, reinforced her beliefs in scary monsters that could overpower humans, and scared her beyond the point of slumber.

The extent to which children continue to experience anxiety as adolescents depends largely on the pressure placed on them by parents, teachers, and peers. Sometimes children and adolescents are pressured to achieve—academically, socially, and physically—according to unrealistic expectations. Intense worry about living up to others' expectations can result in low self-esteem, so it is critical that parents are aware of how their children perceive their expectations.

Be on the lookout for other adults in your child's life who may contribute to your child's anxiety, such as teachers, neighbors, grandparents, siblings, aunts, or uncles. If you can counteract specific situations, you can explain to your child what might be causing her undue confusion and worry. An example would be the softball coach who constantly reminds the players that a loss against a particular team would embarrass your child and the rest of the girls. You could explain to your child that everyone makes mistakes, and no one person on a team is responsible for a win or a loss—it takes a team effort. This would boost your child's confidence that she won't be a failure if she doesn't hit a home run or field the wicked ground ball like a pro. Giving high praise when your child does well yet saying nothing when she has an off day feels the same as criticism to a child. Praise effort, not achievement.

You might make a deal with your partner (or a close friend or family member) to watch what you each say and do that might promote anxiety in your child. A modest amount of anxiety can actually motivate children to achieve; nevertheless, setting realistic expectations is one of the most important steps parents can take to reduce anxiety problems in their child. No child is perfect, and sometimes it is necessary for parents to adjust their expectations. Speaking of being perfect, this next vignette illustrates another guideline.

THE ROLE OF PERFECTIONISM

Parents who consistently set only the highest expectations for their child are setting her up to fail. They create an environment that is all work and no play at a time when children are supposed to make mistakes and celebrate the joys of success in the process of discovering the world on their own terms. The child who grows up in a perfectionistic household becomes prone to developing performance anxiety, as she is constantly fearful of disappointing others. As a result of perpetual fear of failure, she is at increased risk for ulcers, irritable bowel syndrome, nail biting, and physical symptoms related to panic attacks. In terms of anxiety, she is at increased risk for social phobias, panic disorders, and generalized anxiety disorder.

Stain Remover, Pain Remover

We have spent the last two months living in a house that is a complete mess. My husband decided that he wanted to redecorate the kitchen, and that project has snowballed into redecorating the dining room and living room. That means that the entire downstairs is off-limits to our son Nathaniel. There's no place for him to play, because my husband is worried that Nathaniel will ruin some of the work being done. The renovation has cost us a ton of money, and now there's this tension that wasn't there before. I don't know—I guess part of making more money is being able to redecorate the house if you want to, but I didn't ask for a new kitchen, and now I'm caught in the middle of trying to keep my husband from getting upset and helping Nathaniel not be afraid of his dad. He's seen his dad get angry a lot lately, and I can tell that he doesn't want to be alone with him. His own dad!

The other day Nathaniel was drinking this juice he likes. It's a special cherry juice that he had at a friend's house, and it's expensive, kind of hard to find. So he was drinking the juice when his father came home from work. Right away my husband says he can't drink the juice because it might spill on the rug or the new white walls. Nathaniel was pretty upset, so of course I intervened and argued with my husband about it. I suggested that Nathaniel be allowed to drink the juice *outside* the house, either in the yard or at school for a snack. My husband agreed to that, but Nathaniel was still upset that he had to stop drinking his juice. It's like he has no place to play lately since the downstairs is being done, and my husband tells him he always has to "be careful."

Later, after Nathaniel had gone upstairs, I started to go up to check on him, and I noticed a big, red, handprint on the wall in the dining room—the wall that had just been painted. I think he may have done it on purpose, and my husband just "lost it." He hit the roof. How do I get Nathaniel to behave better?

This mother's story illustrates that there may be times when you need to forgive your child for not being perfect. This is not something that needs to be said out loud, but in your own mind. More important, you need to be able to forgive yourself for (1) not creating the perfect home life and (2) not creating the perfect child. The pressure to be the perfect parent is imposed by society, through the media and your peers, and is one additional pressure you may internalize and focus on unconsciously. Research demonstrates that women are probably more susceptible to this pressure than are men, due to the gender roles imposed by society. The accumulation of competing responsibilities, such as earning enough money, providing meals, and maintaining the family's health, result in feelings of resentment that may fester and ultimately cause you to explode when you least expect it. Although the next section pertains primarily to your relationship with your child, it may help you deal with perfectionistic and other stresses between you and your spouse.

REFLECTIVE LISTENING

It is important to remember that every child experiences anxiety reactions in her own individual way. Most children find it calming to be able to describe exactly how their anxiety feels to them, and to explain what they think is causing those feelings. Adults should listen with respect, accepting what the child says as being an accurate representation of what she *thinks* is true, and should avoid making premature judgments. Remember, even if the fear is "all in the child's mind," that does not make it any less real.

Being a good listener does not mean that you should be mute. You need to listen *reflectively*. Sometimes the most important aspect of listening is validating the child's emotions and experiences. Adolescents are more likely to talk—about sex, alcohol, and other important issues—to adults who know how to listen. Certain kinds of responses, such as giving too much advice or pretending to have all the answers, have been shown to block the lines of communication.

The next activity describes five communication skills that are useful to anyone who wants to enhance communication with children or adolescents.

ACTIVITY

◎ 7A ◎

Reflective Listening

Target Age: 5 to 17
Goal: To foster reflective listening, not merely "hearing"
Materials Needed: None

During the course of a conversation with your child, take turns practicing the following skills. One person should begin speaking, and after the conversation has progressed for several minutes, the speaker and listener should switch roles. After a while, there will be no distinction between speaker and listener, because both of you will be sharing and listening in a mutual process of exchange.

1. Rephrase the child's comments to show that you understand. For example: "When you say that you feel sick when you think about playing the piano at your school recital, you mean that your stomach hurts or you might throw up."
2. Watch the child's face and body language. Often your child will assure you that she does not feel sad, but a quivering chin or tearing eyes will tell you otherwise. Your child may deny feeling frightened, but if you put your fingers on her wrist, as a caring gesture, you may find that your child has a racing pulse. When words and body language say two different things, always believe the body language.

3. Give nonverbal support. This may include a smile, a hug, a wink, or a pat on the shoulder; you can nod your head, make eye contact, or hold your child's hand (or wrist).

4. Use the appropriate tone of voice for what you are saying. Remember that your voice tone communicates as clearly as your words. Make sure your tone does not come across as sarcastic or all-knowing.

5. Use encouraging phrases to show your interest and to keep the conversation going. Helpful little phrases, spoken appropriately during pauses in the conversation, can communicate how much you care:

"Oh, really?"

"Tell me more about that."

"Then what happened?"

"That must have made you feel bad."

Reflective listening serves four purposes:

1. It assures your child that you are hearing what she is saying.

2. It persuades your child that you correctly understand what she is saying. (It is sometimes a good idea to ask if your rephrasing is correct.)

3. It allows you a chance to reword your child's statements in ways that are less self-destructive. For example, if your child says, "My sister is a mean witch!" you can say, "You feel your sister is unfair with you." This rephrasing is helpful because being related to someone who is strict allows the child to have a better self-image than being a close relative of a "mean witch."

4. It allows your child to "rehear" and reconsider what she said.

Effective listening takes concentration and practice. Remember, if you are judgmental or critical, your child may decide that you just don't understand. You cannot be a good influence on someone who won't talk to you. Ultimately, support is a fundamental ingredient for enabling your child to develop coping skills and strategies. The child with supportive parents knows that her parents can alleviate her distress or will at least give it their best shot. They will be there for her reliably and unconditionally!

Appendix A

Summary of Activities and Their Goals[1]

In this book we have discussed many ways to decrease your child's anxiety using activities based on the four parts of our COPE model. You can use this appendix as a quick reference: it summarizes all the activities we have presented, as well as their goals.

Chapter Three: COPE Step One: Calming the Nervous System

Activity	Goal
3A. Abdominal Breathing Activity (p. 50)	To learn effective relaxation through correct breathing skills
3B. Getting to Know Your Orange! (p. 54)	To focus on sensory awareness and recognize abilities to use all five senses
3C. Make a Personal Punching Pillow (p. 55)	To release tension in a non-threatening activity
3D. Know Your Own Heart Rate (p. 57)	To be introduced to her heart rate and foster awareness of her ability to both raise and lower it

[1]The authors would like to thank Stacy Phelan for her work on this section.

Activity	Goal
3E. Massage Therapy (p. 60)	To relax muscles and recognize the sensation of relaxation, which can be remembered and recreated on future occasions
3F. Body Sense (p. 62)	To release tensions through the biofeedback technique
3G. Can You Top This? (p. 63)	To stimulate creative and unusual thinking
3H. Scale Those Fears! (p. 65)	To interrupt anxious obsessions and reduce their severity
3I. Pretty Pictures in Your Mind (p. 66)	To develop increased visual ability
3J. Going Under (p.68)	To encourage a state of relaxation and learn how to recreate it in the future
3K. Count Those Sheep (p. 69)	To use repetition as a means of relaxing and focusing on something other than anxiety-provoking situations
3L. "Ouch!" (p. 70)	To use sensory experience to stifle negative thoughts
3M. Ha! (p. 71)	To use laughter as a tension reliever
3N. The Yogic Sponge (p. 73)	To reach a deep state of relaxation and emotional serenity
3O. Evoking Benson's "Relaxation Response" (p. 78)	To foster a relaxation technique that can be used independently, in any environment
3P. Making a Worry Cord (p. 81)	To find a sense of calm through a spiritual connection

Chapter Four: Cope Step Two: Originating an Imaginative Plan

Activity	Goal
4A. The Asking Questions Test of Flexibility (p. 90)	To illustrate the meaning of flexible thinking
4B. The Story-Writing Challenge (p. 93)	To illustrate the imaginative thinking trait known as stimulus freedom
4C. The Nine-Dot Puzzle (p. 96)	To understand the assumption of rules
4D. Becoming Stimulus Free (p. 97)	To cultivate stimulus freedom
4E. The Two-String Problem (p. 100)	To master the concept of functional freedom
4F. Get Your Mind Off It (p. 103)	To use "mindless" activities to practice functional freedom
4G. Mark That Down! (p. 104)	To practice functional freedom while learning new ways to evaluate progress
4H. Digging Deep for Good Ideas (p. 105)	To practice functional freedom by learning to make remote associations
4I. Lateral Thinking = Better Thinking (p. 110)	To have fun thinking in imaginative, unique ways
4J. "The Play's the Thing" (p. 111)	To invent imaginative anti-anxiety plans through role playing
4K. Eavesdropping (p. 114)	To gain a more objective view of his strengths and weaknesses
4L. Why I Am Me (p. 115)	To understand *why* he gets scared, so that he can come up with ways to alleviate his anxiety

Activity	Goal
4M. You Be Me (p. 117)	To help him see his situation from the standpoint of another person
4N. The Empty Chair (p. 118)	To be able to explain his anxious feelings more accurately and to come up with better ways to cope with them
4O. My Memoir (p. 119)	To understand the roots of his anxiety by remembering the first time he felt anxious
4P. Here's What My Family Looks Like (p. 120)	To foster an understanding of his feelings about his family in order to better understand his anxiety
4Q. Winning One Step at a Time (p. 121)	To use small steps as a way to gradually eliminate anxiety
4R. Prepare for the Flood (p. 122)	To lessen anxiety by confronting it directly
4S. Just Floating Along (p. 123)	To learn the technique called floating
4T. My Grokking Rock (p. 124)	To learn to use a "safe place" to relieve anxieties
4U. A Welcoming Lap (p. 125)	To lessen anxiety through the comfort and support of a loved one
4V. A Ritual Your Child Will Come to Love (p. 129)	To involve family members in the design of rituals that can increase the effectiveness of anti-anxiety plans
4W. The Magical Medallion (p. 131)	To use a "magic medallion" to ward off anxious feelings

Chapter Five: COPE Step Three: Persisting in the Face of Obstacles and Failure

Activity	Goal
5A. What's Your Problem? (p. 140)	To deal better with ambiguous situations
5B. "I Guess It's Not So Scary After All" (p. 142)	To see new situations as exciting, not scary
5C. Lessons from a Ring Toss Game (p. 143)	To understand why in life, moderate risks are best
5D. "I Just Can't Do It!" (p. 145)	To learn better ways of thinking about taking moderate risks
5E. Inspiring Stories (p. 149)	To identify with the failures and unflagging determination of real and imaginary heroes and heroines
5F. Stepping Up the Reward Schedule (p. 150)	To enhance motivation through manipulating the reinforcements used
5G. "I Just Need a Good Cry!" (p. 153)	To encourage a more positive attitude toward crying as an appropriate release of tension
5H. Be Like a Seed (p. 154)	To learn an appreciation for the greater rewards that can come from controlling her desires
5I. A Puzzling Solution (p. 156)	To learn to avoid a tendency toward rigid thinking
5J. Where There's a Will, There's a Way (p. 157)	To develop a sense that when one approach to a problem is not working, there are a number of other techniques that might work

Activity	Goal
5K. Slip-Sliding Away in the Movies (p. 158)	To become more aware of the noxious presence of drift
5L. Hang On 'Til the Timer Bell Rings (p. 161)	To practice thought blocking
5M. We're Behind You All the Way (p. 162)	To use family-designed ritual to help strengthen faith in herself, her plan, and a higher power

Chapter Six: COPE Step Four: Evaluating and Adjusting the Plan

Activity	Goal
6A. Three-Times-a-Day Faces Chart (p. 172)	To identify patterns of anxiety, as well as provide an easy-to-use method of formative evaluation for his plan
6B. Goal Thermometer (p. 174)	To create a visible representation of the plan's goal and monitor progress toward reaching that goal
6C. Pulse Counting (p. 176)	To evaluate the progress of the plan by recording heart rate at different times throughout the day
6D. Dream Catchers (p. 178)	To delve into his true feelings about his plan by evaluating his dream
6E. Daily Interviews with a Buddy (p. 179)	To use the support of a good friend in obtaining an objective view of his progress

Activity	Goal
6F. Long Distance (p. 181)	To create a special, valued time to discuss evaluation with a close friend or family member
6G. Muscle Tension Check (p. 182)	To use massage as a tension reliever that promotes creative thinking and decreases anxiety
6H. Here We Go Again (p. 183)	To cope better when symptoms of anxiety recur spontaneously
6I. Check Those Notes (p. 184)	To routinely check on the progress of the current plan
6J. The Peaceful Diary (p. 186)	To more easily and openly describe feelings about the current plan
6K. A Very Personal Letter (p. 187)	To gain a different perspective on the evaluation of his plan
6L. Tape It Now (p. 187)	To produce a detailed account of feelings about anxiety
6M. Candid Camera (p. 188)	To get a more objective view of how he handles himself when he feels anxious
6N. The Video Camera Doesn't Lie! (p. 190)	To view reactions to anxious situations more accurately
6O. The Electronic "Instant Replay" Scoreboard (p. 190)	To imagine a "successful self" in order to increase confidence
6P. Tell Me a Story (p. 191)	To become more objective in summative evaluation
6Q. Hindsight Is Always 20/20 (p. 192)	To recognize aspects of the plan that didn't work well and think of ways to make them better

Activity	Goal
6R. Pretest and Posttest (p. 193)	To quantitatively assess whether anxiety has decreased as a result of the plan

Chapter Seven: How Your Parenting Style Can Help Ease Your Child's Anxiety

Activity	Goal
7A. Reflective Listening (p. 214)	To foster reflective listening, not merely "hearing"

Appendix B

Solutions to Activity Problems

Activity 4C: Solution to the Nine-Dot Puzzle

As you can see in Figure B.1, the solution can be found only by leaving the square. You must extend lines *beyond* the imagined boundary formed by the dots. To do so requires the ability to break free from self-imposed assumptions, to look beyond the obvious. If you or your child were blocked, it was not by a lack of mental agility but by a needlessly narrow point of view.

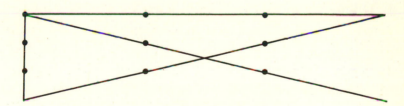

Figure B.1. Solution to the Nine-Dot Puzzle.

Activity 4E: Solution of the Two-String Problem

As shown in Figure B.2, you can use either the clothespin or the mousetrap to solve the problem: attach one or the other to one of the strings; while holding the other string, swing the clothespin or

Figure B.2. Solution to the Two-String Problem.

mousetrap away from you. Catch it as it swings back. Now you can tie the two together readily.

Activity 4H: Answers to the Remote Associations Test

1. jack
2. grade, high
3. box
4. party
5. nut
6. wire
7. net
8. light
9. cut
10. while
11. home
12. bat
13. play
14. numeral
15. black
16. ball

Annotated Bibliography

Some of these books may be out of print, but try searching the Internet; you can probably buy them on-line from such booksellers as amazon.com and barnesandnoble.com.

Books on Self-Control

Baldwin, A. (1955). *Behavior and development in childhood*. New York: Dryden Press.

Bandler, R., & Grinder, J. (1979). *Frogs into princes: Neuro-linguistic programming*. Moab, UT: Real People Press. The authors believe that words can actually effect neurological change. Written in a highly engaging manner; in the words of one reviewer, their book "wears seven-league-boots, and takes personal growth far, far beyond any previous notions."

Bandura, A. (1998). *Self-efficacy*. New York: Freeman. Although this book is written for professionals in psychology, it offers many insights into how human beings achieve their goals.

Blankenstein, K. R., & Polivy, J. (1982). *Self-control and self-modification of emotional behavior*. New York: Plenum. Although a somewhat technical work, there are many good ideas about underlying processes here.

Covey, S. R. (1990). *The seven habits of highly effective people: Powerful lessons in personal change*. New York: Simon & Schuster. Although written about self-control and adults, this book, according to one reviewer, offers many "principles to give us the security to adapt to change, and wisdom and power to take advantage of the opportunities that change creates."

Csikszentmihalyi, M. (1997). *Flow*. New York: Basic Books.

Curtis, R. C. (1989). *Self-defeating behaviors: Experimental research, clinical impressions, and practical implications*. New York: Plenum. Although this reference work presents highly technical research and psychotherapeutic information, the section on practical implications is very useful for parents, counselors, and teachers.

Dacey, J., & Packer, A. (1992). *The nurturing parent*. New York: Simon & Schuster.

DeBono, E. (1992). *Serious creativity*. New York, HarperCollins.

Erikson, E. (1963). *Childhood and society*. New York: Norton.

Garth, M. (1991). *Starbright: Meditations for children*. San Francisco: Harper-Collins. This collection of stories for younger children can, said a reviewer, "help them sleep, develop concentration, awaken creativity, and learn to quiet themselves."

Heinlein, R. (1978). *Stranger in a strange land*. New York: Ace.

Kleinke, C. L. (1998). *Coping with life challenges*. Pacific Grove, CA: Brooks/Cole. Written specifically to deal with difficult situations such as death and pain, this book offers coping strategies and self-scoring assessment questionnaires that are quite useful.

Logue, A. W. (1995). *Self-control: Waiting until tomorrow for what you want today*. Englewood Cliffs, NJ: Prentice Hall. This book focuses on the behaviorist approach. The theory part of the book is somewhat jargonistic, and it would help if you know something about psychology. The exercises, however, are easier to read and give very good advice.

Martin, G., & Pear, J. (1996). *Behavior modification: What it is and how to do it*. Englewood Cliffs, NJ: Prentice Hall. This textbook assumes no prior knowledge of psychology. It is an excellent source on this powerful technique for achieving self-control.

Mednick, S. (1962). The associative basis of the creative process. *Psychological Review, 69*, 220–232.

Satir, V. (1986). *I*. Palo Alto, CA: Science and Behavior Books.

Selye, H. (1974). *Stress without distress*. Philadelphia: Lippincott. The discoverer of the general adaptation syndrome, Selye says that his book explains "how to achieve a rewarding lifestyle, in harmony with the laws of nature, by using stress as a positive force for personal achievement and happiness."

Torrance, E. P. (1995). *Why fly?* Norwood, NJ: Ablex.

The books on the following list were written primarily for teachers and counselors, but they contain many helpful ideas for parents, too.

Chamberlin, S. R. (1996). *The strategies of self control used by personnel who work with adolescents*. Doctoral dissertation, Boston College, Chestnut Hill, MA. (Available in most college libraries.)

Furman, E. (1998). *Self-control and mastery in early childhood: Helping young children grow*. Madison, CN: International Universities Press.

Gootman, M. E. (1997). *The caring teacher's guide to discipline: Helping young students learn self-control, responsibility, and respect*. Thousand Oaks, CA: Corwin Press.

Gordon, T. (1989). *Teaching children self-discipline . . . at home and at school*. New York: Random House.

Heckhausen, J., & Dweck, C. S. (1998). *Motivation and self-regulation across the life span*. New York: Cambridge University Press.

Maag, J. (1998). *Teaching children and youth self-control: Applications of perceptual control theory*. Reston, VA: Council for Children with Behavioral Disorders.

Ridley, D., & Walther, B. (1995). *Creating responsible learners: The role of a positive classroom environment*. Washington, DC: American Psychological Association.

Schunk, D. H. (1998). *Self-regulated learning: From teaching to self-reflective practice*. New York: Guilford Press.

Shapiro, L. E. (1995). *In control: A book of games to teach children self-control skills*. King of Prussia, PA: Center for Applied Psychology.

Zimmerman, B. J. (1996). *Developing self-regulated learners: Beyond achievement to self-efficacy*. Washington, DC: American Psychological Association.

Books on Anxiety

Austin, V. (1998). *Free yourself from fear: Self-hypnosis for anxiety, panic attacks, and phobias*. Hammersmith, London: Thorsons. Written in an engaging style, this book discusses the benefits of hypnosis as an effective treatment for anxiety and anxiety-related disorders.

Benson, H., & Klipper, M. Z. (1992). *The relaxation response*. New York: Wings Books.

Brenner, A. (1984). *Helping children cope with stress*. San Francisco: New Lexington Press. This book discusses the numerous sources of stress in a child's life and presents coping strategies. The author distinguishes between healthy and self-destructive coping strategies and presents recommendations for future research in this area.

Brown, J. L. (1995). *No more monsters in the closet: Teaching your children to overcome everyday fears and phobias*. New York: Prince. A simple and straightforward approach for parents or others who know an anxious child, this book presents techniques and explanations for many of childhood's fears and anxieties. Attention is paid to specific age groups and appropriate ideas for each group.

Burns, D. D. (1980). *Feeling good: The new mood therapy*. New York: Signet. Introducing the concept of cognitive therapy, the author describes how changing the way a person thinks can alter his or her mood. This approach also attempts to reduce distorted perceptions that might contribute to a person's anxieties.

Curtis, J., & Detert, R. (1998). *How to relax*. New York: HarperCollins.

DuPont, R. L., Spencer, E. D., & DuPont, C. M. (1998). *The anxiety cure: An eight-step program for getting well*. New York: Wiley. This book presents an eight-step program for relief of anxiety symptoms. There are many good ideas and suggestions here for parents and others.

Field, T. M. (1998). "Massage therapy effects." *American-Psychologist, 53*(12), 1270–1281.

Field, T. M., et al. (1998). "Elder retired volunteers benefit from giving massage therapy to infants." *Journal of Applied Gerontology, 17*(2), 229–239.

Garber, S. W., Garber, M. D., & Spizman, R. F. (1993). *Monsters under the bed and other childhood fears: Helping your child overcome anxieties, fears, and phobias*. New York: Villard Books. This book addresses both coping with and overcoming fears. The authors address specific fears as they occur developmentally across childhood, and the text is written in an enjoyable and thorough manner.

Gerzon, R. (1998). *Finding serenity in the age of anxiety*. New York: Bantam Books. This book approaches the concepts of anxiety, stress, and fear from a new perspective. The author argues that these feelings are natural and may ultimately lead to serenity if they are understood and used in a healthy manner.

Hallowell, E. M. (1997). *Worry: Hope and help for a common condition*. New York: Ballantine Books. Using personal experiences and case studies, Dr. Hallowell discusses all kinds of worry and the underlying causes that promote it. Infusing his writing with compassion and humor, Dr. Hallowell presents a way for worriers to channel their worry in a more healthy and practical way.

Manassis, K. (1996). *Keys to parenting your anxious child*. New York: Barron's. This book is a practical guide for parents of anxious children. The author describes how to recognize anxiety in your child, and offers advice about how parents can help their anxious child in the context of the home and school.

Noyes, R., Jr., & Hoehn-Saric, R. (1998). *The anxiety disorders*. New York: Cambridge University Press. Although this book is written for professionals in psychology, it is an excellent resource for anyone interested in anxiety disorders, particularly the latest clinical classifications for each disorder. Comprehensive and well written, this book provides detailed information about many disorders, including diagnostic criteria and treatment techniques.

Philadelphia Child Guidance Center. (1993). *Your child's emotional health: The middle years*. Old Tappan, NJ: Macmillan. This book presents the stages of children's emotional development from age six to age thirteen. It discusses such issues as fear, depression, and school, and gives advice about when to handle problems at home and when to seek professional help.

Robbins, J., & Fisher, D. (1972). *Tranquility without pills: All about transcendental meditation*. The authors of this book present a relaxation technique that is an effective way to relieve stress without medication. The book discusses the benefits of the relaxation technique and provides case studies to illustrate various concepts.

Ross, J. (1994). *Triumph over fear: A book of help and hope for people with anxiety, panic attacks, and phobias*. New York: Bantam Books. The author of this book uses case histories and personal experience to help people deal with anxiety disorders. It also discusses the development and treatment of disorders.

Sarafino, E. P. (1986). *The fears of childhood: A guide to recognizing and reducing fearful states in children*. New York: Human Sciences Press. This book is written for parents, teachers, and students of psychology who have an interest in understanding how to help a child when fears arise. Drawing on his own research, Dr. Sarafino describes methods for preventing and reducing fears.

Shaw, M. A. (1995). *Your anxious child: Raising a healthy child in a frightening world*. New York: Birch Lane Press. Parents of an anxious child will appreciate this book, written specifically to help them identify and understand anxiety in their children. One of the goals of this book is to help parents feel less anxious themselves so that they may better help their anxious child.

Silva, J., & Miele, P. (1977). *The Silva mind control method*. New York: Simon & Schuster. The founder of the Silva Mind Control method presents his meditation technique. This method can be used to overcome stress, release creative impulses, and transform bad habits into good ones.

Tappan, F. M. (1988). *Healing massage techniques: Holistic, classic, and emerging methods*. Norwalk, CN: Appleton & Lange.

Wilson, R. R. (1986). *Don't panic: Taking control of anxiety attacks*. New York: HarperCollins. This book explains the causes and effects of panic attacks. The author also outlines a program for overcoming panic and managing fears.

Wolpe, J., & Wolpe, D. (1988). *Life without fear: Anxiety and its cure*. Oakland, CA: New Harbinger. This book draws a distinction between useful and useless fears and discusses how habits are formed that can both foster and reduce anxiety. It describes different methods of treatment to provide readers with options should they decide to seek professional help.

About the Authors

John S. Dacey, Ph.D., is professor and chair of the master's program in developmental psychology at Boston College. He is the recipient of numerous grants for the study of the cognitive development in adolescents and adults. He is the author of nine textbooks on child, adolescent, and lifespan development and two books on parenting. Dacey is also a psychotherapist; for thirteen years he was codirector of a weekend camp at which creative problem-solving skills were taught to teenagers.

Lisa B. Fiore, Ph.D., teaches courses in developmental and educational psychology at Boston College and Curry College. Her background as an early childhood educator has fostered her research in Head Start centers and her work in counseling parents of young children.

Index

A

Abdominal breath control, 49–53. *See also* Calming, of nervous system: physical methods for

Abdominal breathing activity, 50–52, 217

Abdominal discomfort, 35

Abnormal brain activity, 8

Acrophobia, 30

ACTH hormone, 47

Adaption response, 46, 47

Adrenaline, 8–9, 44, 46, 47, 151–152

Aerobic exercise, 56–58. *See also* Calming, of nervous system: physical methods for

Age, affects of, 13–15

Agora, 32

Agoraphobia: description of, 32–33; and panic disorder, 34–35. *See also* Anxiety disorders, in children and adolescents

Alarm reaction, 8–9, 45–46

"Alfred G.," 36–37

Amapthophobia, 30

Ambiguity: and familiarity-stress continuum, 141; persistence in face of, 138–142; toleration of, as two-part problem, 139–140

Animal phobia, 29, 30. *See also* Specific phobia

Antianxiety plans: floating strategy for, 123–124; flooding strategy for, 122–123; safe place strategy for, 124–126; successive approximation strategy for, 121–122

Anticipatory anxiety, 36, 37

Anxiety: among Caribbean children, 11–13; anticipatory, 36, 37; behaviorist perspective on, 17; cognitive perspective on, 20–21; COPE method for, 3, 21–24; coping skills for, 2–4; current therapeutic perspectives on, 15–21; at different ages and stages, 13–15; family systems perspective on, 17–18; *versus* fear or worry, 6; major causes of, 8–13; nature of, 5–6; as problem, 6–7; psychoanalytic perspective on, 16–17

Anxiety disorders, in children and adolescents: and agoraphobia, 32–34; eight types of, 28–41; four problems central to, 2; generalized (GAD), 37–38; and obsessive-compulsive disorder (OCD), 40–41; and panic disorder, 34–37; and posttraumatic stress disorder (PTSD), 39; and separation anxiety, 38; and social phobia, 31–32; and specific phobia, 29–31

Appetite, decreased, 9

Arndell, J., 11–13

Asking questions test, of flexibility, 90–93, 219; categories for scoring of, 91–92
Astraphobia, 30
Authoritarian parenting, 200. *See also* Parenting style
Authoritative parenting, 202–203. *See also* Parenting styles
Auto, 137
Autogenic training, 72–77. *See also* Calming, of nervous system: combined physical and mental methods for
Autotelic personality, 137

B
Baldwin, A., 203
Bandura, A., 17
Bank of goodwill, 82–83
Baumrind, D., 199–203
Beck, A., 20
Behaviorist theory, 17. *See also* Anxiety: current therapeutic perspectives on
Benson, H., 77, 218
Bergman, I., 19
Biofeedback, 61–62. *See also* Calming, of nervous system: physical methods for
Biological factors, in anxiety, 8–10
Biopsychosocial model: biological factors in, 8–10; and parenting style, 198; psychological factors in, 10; social factors in, 10–11; for understanding human traits, 8–13
Blood-clotting ability, increased, 9
Blood-injection-injury phobia, 29, 30. *See also* Specific phobia
Blood vessels, constriction/dilation of, 9
Body language, 214
Body sense, 62, 218. *See also* Biofeedback
Breath: abdominal control of, 49–53, 217; and panic, 50–52; shortness of, 35
Buddhist prayer, 79. *See also* Prayer

C
Calming, of nervous system: activities and goals for, 217–218; alarm reaction and, 46–49; combined physical and mental methods for, 72–79; in COPE method, 21–22; mental methods for, 63–72; physical methods for, 49–62; spiritual methods for, 79–83
Carbon dioxide, 50
Caribbean culture, 11–13
Catastrophizing, 160
Centering, 170–171
Charts, use of, 171–177. *See also* Formative evaluation
Checklists, use of, 183–186. *See also* Formative evaluation
Chest pain, 35
Childhood and Society (Erikson), 16
Chronophobia, 30
Cognitive restructuring, 20
Cognitive theory, 20–21. *See also* Anxiety: current therapeutic perspectives on
Concentrating, difficulty in, 37
Confidence, 204
Control: fear of, 35; loss of, in agoraphobia, 32; sense of, 12, 203
Cooperative behavior, 202
COPE method: four steps of, 21–24; role of parents in, 3; step four of, 165–196, 222–224; step one of, 43–83, 217–218; step three of, 135–164, 221–222; step two of, 85–134, 219–220
Coping skills, 2
Courage: and increased reinforcement, 150; increasing reward schedule for enhancement of, 150–151; and inspiring stories, 149–150; in persistence, 147–153
Creativity, 95, 203, 204.
Crying: encouraging positive attitude toward, 153, 221; release of adrenaline in, 151–152; societal taboo against male, 151–152
Csikszentmihalyi, M., 137

Cultural influence, 11, 204–207
Curtis, J., 48

D

Dacey, J. S., 18, 21, 25, 59, 94, 112, 177, 203–204
Dacey-Fiore Anxiety Questionnaire, 193–195
Danger, possibility of, 10
deBono, E., 108
Delaware River, 18
Demandingness, 199, 203. *See also* Parenting style
Democratic parenting, 203
Depression, 3
Desire, 136
Detachment, from self, 35
Detert, R., 48
Diaphragm, 50, 51. *See also* Abdominal breath control
Diary. *See* Journal writing
Digestive ability, decreased, 9
Disengaged parenting, 200–201
Disorder, definition of, 27
Distraction, 69–70. *See also* Calming, of nervous system: mental methods for
Dizziness, 35
Draw-a-Person Test, 119–120, 177–178
Drawings, 177–179. *See also* Formative evaluation
Dream catchers, 178–179, 222. *See also* Formative evaluation
Drift: avoidance of, 158–159; definition of, 136
Dry mouth, 9
Dvořák, A., 137
Dying, fear of, 36

E

Eating disorders, 11
Eating habits, 9–10
Eavesdropping Activity, 114–115, 219
Edison, T., 137, 154
Emotions, venting, 55–56
Empathy, 201

Empty chair activity, 118–119
Encouraging phrases, 215
Environment, 8
"Erica M.," 33–34
Erikson, E., 16
Erythrophobia, 30
Ethnicity, role of, in evaluation of plans, 169–170
Evaluation: activities and goals for, 222–224; formative type of, 168–169; of plan, in COPE method, 21, 23–24; role of gender and ethnicity in, 169–170; summative type of, 169. *See also* Formative evaluation; Summative evaluation
Expectations, 210–211
Eyesight, sharpening of, 9

F

Faces chart, three-times-a-day, 172–173, 222
Faith, 159–164
Familiarity, and stress, 141–142. *See also* Ambiguity
Family-designed ritual: benefits of, 127–128; dimensions of, 126–127; three rules for, 130; use of basic elements in, 128–129
Family systems therapy, 17–18. *See also* Anxiety: current therapeutic perspectives on
Fear: and age level, 13–15; *versus* anxiety, 6–7; of fear, in agoraphobia, 32–33
Fear scale, 64–65, 218. *See also* Calming, of nervous system: mental methods for
Feedback, 23
Feelings, focus on, 20
Field, T. M., 59
Fight-or-flight response, 9, 22, 44, 45, 47, 151
Fiore, L., 4, 52, 185
Flexibility, asking questions test of, 90–93, 219
Flexibility strategy, 90–93
Floating strategy, 123–124

Flooding strategy, 122–123
Formative evaluation: interview with friend in, 179–182; journal writing in, 186–188; therapist for, 182–183; as type of plan assessment, 168–169; use of charts in, 171–177; use of checklists in, 183–186; use of drawings in, 177–179; use of photography for, 179–182
Francis, Saint (of Assisi), 80
Freud, S., 16
Friends, use of, in evaluation of plan, 179–182, 222
Friese, B. H., 126–127
Fromm, E., 159
Functional freedom, 100–108

G

GAD. See Generalized Anxiety Disorder
Galvanic skin response (GSR), 61–62
Gataphobia, 30
Gender, role of, in evaluation of plans, 169–170
Generalized adaptation syndrome, 47, 82
Generalized anxiety disorder (GAD), 37–38, 59
Genes, 8
Goal thermometer, 174–175, 222. See also Formative evaluation
God, 23, 79
Goodness-of-fit, 205
Goodwill, bank of. See Bank of goodwill
Gratification, valuing delay of, 155. See also Persistence
Great Spirit, 23
Greeks, ancient, 128
Grokking rock, 124–125, 220
GSR. See Galvanic skin response
Guilt, feelings of, 198

H

Habit: anxious children as creatures of, 138; and avoidance of drift, 158

Hair, raising of, 9
Hallowell, E. M., 48
Harpaxophobia, 30
Heart rate, increased, 8, 35, 46, 47, 217. See also Target heart rate (THR)
Heinlein, R., 124
Higher power, 23
Himalayas, 78
Hippocrates, 32
Hormonal imbalances, 8
How to Relax (Curtis and Detert), 48
Humor, 71–72. See also Calming, of nervous system: mental methods for
Hurricane Andrew, 59
Hurricane Luis, 11–12
Hylophobia, 30
Hyperadrenalism, 47
Hyperventilation, 9, 47, 49–50, 51
Hypervigilance, 9, 10, 45–46
Hypochondria, 30
Hypoglycemia, 47

I

Imaginative allies, use of, 110–113
Imaginative mind, nature of, 133–134
Imaginative plan: origination of, 21, 22–23. See also Imaginative problem-solving
Imaginative problem-solving: activities and goals for, 219–220; and family-designed ritual, 126–131; flexibility strategy for, 90–93; functional freedom strategy for, 100–108; and gaining insights into child's problem, 113–120; guidelines for, 132–134; lateral thinking strategy for, 108–110; remote associations strategy for, 105–108; sociodrama strategy for, 110–113; stimulus freedom strategy for, 93–100
Independence, 202
Indian Princesses, 4–5
Inferiority, sense of, 16
Inner talk, 12

Inspiration, 149–150, 221
Internalization, of parental anxieties, 207–208
Interpretation, faulty, 20–22
Irritability, 37
Itinerant artist, 112–113

J

"Jake," 165–167
"James T.," 40–41
Journal of Family Psychology, 126–127
Journal writing, 186–188, 223. *See also* Formative evaluation

K

Kenny, Sister E., 148–149
Klee, P., 137
Kline, C. A., 126–127

L

Lateral thinking, 108–110, 219
Lateral Thinking (deBono), 108
Lightheadedness, 35
Logic, faulty, 20

M

Magical medallion, 131, 220
Mantra, 77–78
"Marilyn T.," 40–41
Massage, 59–61, 182, 218. *See also* Calming, of nervous system: physical methods for
Medical student syndrome, 41
Meditation, 77–79. *See also* Calming, of nervous system: combined physical and mental methods for
Mednick, S., 106, 107
Memoir activity, 119, 220
Mensch, 82
Mental ability, decreased, 9
Mental errors, 47
Michelangelo, 137
Mistaken thinking, 7, 21. *See also* Perception, faulty
Misunderstanding, 7, 22. *See also* Interpretation, faulty

Modeling: behaviorist concept of, 17; of moderate risk-taking behaviors, 146–147
Moore, M., 107
Motor ability, increased, 9
Muscle tension: unusual, 37, 223; use of massage for, 182
Mutism, selective, 31–32

N

Natural environment phobia, 29, 30. *See also* Specific phobia
Nature, 8
Nausea, 35
Necrophobia, 30
Neill, A. S., 201
Nervous system: and alarm reaction, 46–49; calming of, 21, 22, 49–83, 217–218; "high-wired," 10
Nine-dot puzzle, 96–97, 219
Nonverbal support, 215
Numbness, 35
Nurture, 8
Nurturing Parent, The (Dacey and Packer), 203
Nurturing parenting, 203–204

O

Objectivity, 189–193
Obsessive-compulsive disorder (OCD), 40–41
Obsessive pulse-taker, 177
OCD. *See* Obsessive-compulsive disorder
Open-mindedness, 155–158
Origination of imaginative plan. *See* Imaginative problem-solving
Oxygen, 50

P

Packer, A., 203–204
Pallor, increased, 9
Panic attack: and generalized anxiety disorder, 37; and panic disorder, 34–35
Panic disorder, 34–37

Pantrophobia, 30

Paradoxical thinking, 63–64. *See also* Calming, of nervous system: mental methods for

Parenting style: authoritarian, 200; authoritative, 202–203; contribution of, to child's development, 11; cultural context for, 204–207; definition of, 198–199; demandingness in, 199; democratic, 203; and disengaged parenting, 200–201; effect of child's temperament on, 204–207; and internalization of parental anxieties, 207–208; nurturing, 203–204; patterns of behavior used in, 11; permissive, 200–202; reflective listening in, 213–216, 224; responsiveness in, 199–200; role of perfectionism in, 211–213; validation in, 213

Perceived threat. *See* Threats: perception of

Perception, faulty, 7, 21

Perfectionism, 11, 211–213

Permissive parenting, 200–202. *See also* Parenting style

Persistence: acquiring sense of courage for, 147–153; activities and goals for, 221–222; and avoidance of drift, 158–159; avoidance of rigid thinking for, 155–158; delay of gratification in, 153–155; in face of obstacles and failure, 21, 23; and imagination, 137–138; learning to handle risks and, 143–147; sense of faith for, 159–164; toleration of ambiguity in, 138–142

Personality, autotelic, 137

Perspective, 3

Philips, K., 11–13

Photography, 188–189. *See also* Formative evaluation

Piaget, J., 15

Plans: evaluating and adjusting of, 23; how to evaluate, 167–169; origination of imaginative, 22–23

Possibility, sensitivity to, 10

Posttraumatic stress disorder (PTSD), 31, 39, 41, 59. *See also* Anxiety disorders, in children and adolescents

Prayer, 79–82; rhythmic approach to, 79–80; substantive approach to, 80–81. *See also* Calming, of nervous system: spiritual methods for

Pretest and posttest, 193–196, 224

Process, *versus* product, 154

Psychoanalysis, 16–17. *See also* Anxiety: current therapeutic perspectives on

Psychological factors, in anxiety, 10

Psychology, 15–21

PTSD. *See* Posttraumatic stress disorder

Pulse counting, 176, 222. *See also* Formative evaluation

Punishment, 200

Q

Qualitative feeling, 180

Quantitative feelings, 180

Queasiness, 9

R

Reflective listening: in parenting style, 213–214; five communication skills for, 214–215; purposes served by, 215

Reinforcement, increased, 150

Relaxation response: abdominal breathing and, 50; definition of, 77; evocation of, 78–79; four steps in activation of, 77

Relaxation Response, The (Benson), 77, 218

Remote Association Test, 106

Remote associations, 105–108

Repetition, 69–71, 78–79

Rephrasing, of child's comments, 214

Respect, 202

Responsibility, sense of, 203

Responsiveness, 199–200. *See also* Parenting styles

Restlessness, 37

Reward schedule, 150–151, 221

Rigid thinking, avoidance of, 155–158

Ring toss game, 143–144, 221

Ripple, R., 94

Risks: learning to handle, 143–147; and modeling moderate risk taking, 146–147; taking moderate, 144–146

Ritual, definition of, 126

Robert E. and Katherine T. MacArthur Fellowship (MacArthur Award), 149

"Rock-a-Bye-Baby" (lullaby), 208–209

Roman Catholicism (prayer), 79, 128. *See also* Prayer

Rousseau, J.-J., 201

Rozen, H., 85–87

S

Safe place strategy, 124–126

Salivation, decreased, 9

San Bernardino Mountains, 4

Satir, V., 17

School phobia, 14

Selective mutism, 31–32. *See also* Social phobia

Self, detachment from, 35

Self-consciousness, 168

Self-control, 153–154, 202

Self-esteem, 201

Self-hypnosis, 67–68. *See also* Calming, of nervous system: mental methods for

Selye, H., 47, 82–83

Sensory awareness, 53–54. *See also* Calming, of nervous system: physical methods for

Separation anxiety, 13, 38. *See also* Anxiety disorders, in children and adolescents

Sex, decreased interest in, 9

Sharing, 201

Shyness, 31

Silent affliction, 2

Simple phobia. *See* Specific phobia

Situational phobia, 29, 30. *See also* Specific phobia

Skinner, B. F., 17

Sleep disturbance, 37

Sleeping routines, 9–10

Social context, importance of, 10–13

Social phobia, 31–32. *See also* Anxiety disorders, in children and adolescents

Social skills, 203

Sociodrama, 110–113

Specific phobia: definition of, 29, 31; types of, 30. *See also* Anxiety disorders, in children and adolescents

Spiritual beings, punishment by, 12

Spiritual help, categories of, 162

St. Maarten, 11–13

St. Thomas Church, 25

Still, W., 136

Stimulation, 9–10

Stimulus freedom, 93–100, 139, 219

Story-writing challenge, 93–94, 219

Stranger in a Strange Land (Heinlein), 124

Stress: as keyword for World Wide Web, 61; neurological response to, 22; recognizing the presence of, 48; relationship of, to familiarity, 141–142

Stressors, five categories of, 48

Substance abuse, 3

Successive approximation strategy, 121–122

Summative evaluation: and Dacey-Fiore anxiety questionnaire, 193–196; as dimension of plan assessment, 169; objectivity in, 169–193

Summerhill (Neill), 201

Supernatural creatures, 12–13, 14

Supportive surfaces, 58–59. *See also* Calming, of nervous system: physical methods for

Sweating, 9, 35

Symptoms, anxiety, 189–190

T

Talking stick, 130
Target heart rate (THR), 56, 57–58
Telos, 137
Temperament, 8, 204–207
Tension, overall feeling of, 9
Therapeutic perspectives, 15–21
Therapist, use of, in formative evaluation, 182–183
Therapy, message. *See also* Calming, of nervous system: physical methods for
Thought, cognitive focus on, 20
Thought blocking, 160, 161
THR. *See* Target heart rate
Threats: perception of, 5–6; use of, 209
Time, role of, in resistance to change, 158–159
Tingling, 35
Tiredness, 37
Tone of voice, 215
Torrance, E. P., 147
Training, autogenic, 72–77
Traits, human, biopsychosocial model for understanding, 8–13
Transcendental meditation, 77–78
Transference, 16–17
Trauma, history of: and posttraumatic stress disorder, 39; in specific phobia, 29, 31
Trembling, 9, 35
Triakaidekaphobia, 30

Trust, 204
Tubman, H., 135–136
Two-string problem, 100–102, 219

U

Unknown. *See* Ambiguity
Unreality, feelings of, 35

V

Validation, parental, 213
Venting, of emotions, 55–56. *See also* Calming, of nervous system: physical methods for
Verbal ability, decreased, 9
Vertical thinking, 108–109
Vigilance, 45
Visualization, 66–67. *See also* Calming, of nervous system: mental methods for
Voice: heightening of, 9; tone of, 215
Vulnerability, perception of, 45

W

Weeks, C., 123
"What-ifs," *versus* anxiety, 3–4
Worry: about worry, 37; *versus* anxiety, 6; and stress, 48
Worry: Hope and Help for a Common Condition (Hallowell), 48
Worry cord, 81–82, 218

Z

Zoophobia, 30